PCs

FOR BUSY PEOPLE

About the Author...

David Einstein is a technology reporter for the *San Francisco Chronicle*, specializing in personal computers. He has also been a reporter for the *Los Angeles Times* and the Associated Press. Dave lives in Petaluma, California, with his wife, two sons, two dogs, and several PCs.

PCs

FOR BUSY PEOPLE

David Einstein

Osborne/**McGraw-Hill**

Berkeley / New York / St. Louis / San Francisco / Auckland / Bogotá
Hamburg / London / Madrid / Mexico City / Milan / Montreal / New Delhi
Panama City / Paris / São Paulo / Singapore / Sydney / Tokyo / Toronto

Osborne/**McGraw-Hill**
2600 Tenth Street
Berkeley, California 94710
U.S.A.

For information on translations or book distributors outside the U.S.A., or to
arrange bulk purchase discounts for sales promotions, premiums, or fundraisers,
please contact Osborne **McGraw-Hill** at the above address.

PCs for Busy People

1234567890 DOC 99876

ISBN 0-07-882210-6

Acquisitions Editor: Joanne Cuthbertson
Project Editor: Nancy McLaughlin
Technical Editor: Heidi Steele
Proofreader: Stefany Otis
Indexer: David Heiret
Computer Designers: Roberta Steele, Leslee Bassin
Graphic Artist: Lance Ravella
Technical Illustration: Charles Solway
Series and Cover Design: Ted Mader Associates
Series Illustration: Daniel Barbeau
Quality Control: Joe Scuderi

Contents at a glance

Contents

Part 2

Acknowledgments

A class act is easy to spot. You see it when the Dallas Cowboys make a big play for a touchdown, and you hear it when the Chicago Symphony launches into Mahler. It's teamwork in action, a combination of enthusiasm, talent, and singleness of purpose that runs through an organization. Such true professionalism is rare, and when you've been a part of it, you experience a certain glow. That's the way I felt with the people at Osborne/McGraw-Hill.

When Joanne Cuthbertson approached me about writing *PCs for Busy People,* it was immediately clear that she was committed to setting a new standard for books in this field. Her excitement was infectious, and it stayed with me throughout the project. She also exhibited the kind of grace under pressure that a writer dreams of in an editor. Thanks, Joanne, for making me feel like a part of the Osborne family.

As the book started coming together, I became aware of the crucial role that other people were playing in making my work the best it could be. Nancy McLaughlin, my project editor/copy editor, probably deserves to share the byline with me. She has a lovely touch with the language, and her suggestions never failed to improve the writing.

The unsung hero of the book probably is the technical editor, Heidi Steele. It took someone with extraordinary knowledge of personal computers to tackle the technical issues raised in a book that covers as many hardware and software issues as this one. Heidi was more than up to the task.

The Busy People books are blessed with a unique design that can't help but liven up anyone's writing. Ted Mader and Mary Jo Kovarik of Ted Mader Associates, along with the Osborne production team, all should stand and take a bow for their efforts in making this book the best-looking of its kind on the market. And special kudos to artist Dan Barbeau, whose characters cavort through these pages.

Hey, Heidi, I didn't forget you! Editorial assistant Heidi Poulin was always there when I needed her, which was often.

No book succeeds without great marketing, and Osborne has that in abundance. Let's hear it for Kendal Anderson, Anne Ellingsen, Susan Bergesen, and Susan Charles; thanks to their spreading the word, the Busy People books have garnered the attention they deserve.

Lastly, I'd like to acknowledge someone who doesn't work for Osborne, but who played perhaps the most crucial role of all. My wife, Diane. She kept my spirits up and refused to let me succumb to writer's block, and she didn't complain once, even though I was glued to the computer for something like twelve straight weekends.

Looking back, I'm amazed at how smoothly this book came together. But that's what happens when you're dealing with true professionals.

PRIORITY!

Introduction

Using a personal computer is a lot like driving a car. Most people don't understand the intricacies of an internal combustion engine, and guess what? They don't care. All they want is to get from here to there as quickly and comfortably as possible. The same goes for the PC. Today's busy professional or hard-working student doesn't really care about bits and bytes. They just want to be able to write that report in time for tomorrow's meeting, or fax off the latest sales figures, or print some cool stuff off the Internet. In short, they want the PC to work for them. If you fall into this category, you're not alone. Most people in today's fast-paced society don't have time to learn about technology.

Fortunately, Osborne/McGraw-Hill has come up with a solution: its *Busy People* series. The aim of this book is to provide a level of comfort and familiarity that will let you get the most out of your computer system, whether you use it for work, home finance, or entertainment.

I KNOW YOU'RE IN A HURRY, SO...

Let's get right down to business. Personal computers can already be found in more than one-third of all American homes, but few people really understand much about them. They do know, however, that a PC usually costs more than the family TV and stereo combined. We know that you want to get your money's worth out of your computer—and that you're hoping it will make your life easier in the bargain. With those goals in mind, we've created this book to help you:

- Cut through the technobabble
- Decide which PC is best for you
- Shop wisely and get the most for your money
- Set up your system for its optimal health—and yours
- Get under the hood to expand your PC or upgrade it
- Make the most of Windows
- Determine what software you need, and use it efficiently
- Learn about multimedia
- Merge smoothly onto the information superhighway

Not everything in this book will apply to everybody. If you already have a PC that's Windows 95-compatible, advice on buying a new system probably won't be crucial. Still, the nuts-and-bolts information on different kinds of systems should be helpful down the line, when you replace your current system—or buy an additional PC.

And let's get something clear while we're still at the gate: This book deals with IBM-compatible PCs—that is, systems that use Intel chips (or clones of them) and Microsoft Windows 95. If you have an Apple Macintosh, you're reading the wrong book. Keep an eye out for Don Crabb's *Macs for Busy People*, due to hit the shelves in a big way later this summer.

STAYING AHEAD OF THE CURVE

Even if you've just bought a new PC, technology is moving so quickly that within a couple of years, you're going to have to either upgrade your machine or buy a new one. In large part, this is due to something called Moore's Law—named after Gordon Moore, a pioneer who helped start Intel Corporation. He postulated that the power of computer chips would double every 18 months, and so it has. Such rapid evolution has been a blessing, because it's ultimately given us PCs that are more powerful than all the hardware Mission Control had when we landed our first men on the moon. On the other hand, it means that today's state-of-the-art PC is tomorrow's dinosaur. This book will help you weave your way through the technological revolution and come out a winner.

Throughout the book, various points of interest will appear in margin notes like this one.

THINGS YOU MIGHT WANT TO KNOW ABOUT THIS BOOK

You can read this book in any order. It's a resource book, not a novel. (If anybody reads it cover to cover, it probably means that their flight has been delayed and the airport is closed due to bad weather.) PC novices probably should start at the beginning, but people with more confidence or experience can hop around. (If you're not up to snuff on Windows 95, for instance, you might want to tackle Chapter 4 first.)

Here's a rundown of some of the elements you'll encounter as you read:

Fast Forwards

At the beginning of each chapter, you'll find a Fast Forward section. These sections are ideal for people who are impatient, or more experienced with PCs, or both. They describe the major themes of the chapter in just a few words, and provide page references to more in-depth treatments of each topic within the chapter. Some readers will find that the Fast Forwards are all they need on certain subjects.

Habits & Strategies

This feature, which pops up any time you see a fellow sitting at a chessboard, suggests techniques that can save you time and make working with your PC more enjoyable and less frustrating. Good ideas such as making it a habit to back up your data files. These habit-forming margin notes also give you the big picture and help you plan ahead.

Shortcuts

If there's one thing busy people need, it's the ability to do things more quickly. When there's a way to do something that's maybe not as conventional as the method described in the text, but that is *faster*, I'll tell you about it in the margin. Just look for the man jumping over the fence with his tie flying in the breeze.

Cautions

Whether you're dealing with PC hardware or software, it's possible to make a mistake and spend hours trying to retrace your steps. It's also possible to damage your system, which can be costly. The guy in the hard hat will warn you of possible pitfalls, and point out how you can avoid them.

Definitions

Where I can't avoid using computer jargon, I'll usually explain it the first time it occurs in the text. Short definitions of some common computer terms can also be found in the margins; you'll recognize them by the bodybuilding dude. Learn to use these terms wisely, and you'll be a hit at the next cocktail party.

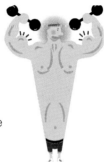

Step by Steps

To help you master more complicated tasks, the flashy blue Step by Step boxes will walk you through selected procedures, using helpful illustrations.

LET'S DO IT

Computer technology isn't rocket science. Actually, it's more complicated than that. But it doesn't take a computer genius to get the most out a PC; even a busy person can do it. Trust me on this one.

Part 1

HARDWARE

Everything You Never Wanted to Know (but Probably Should) About PCs

FAST FORWARD

THINK FAST ➤ *pp. 8-9*
The brains of the PC is the *microprocessor,* also known as the *chip.*
If all you want to do is word processing and surfing the Internet,
a 486-class microprocessor should be fine. But if you're into
multimedia or heavy graphics, don't settle for less than a Pentium-
level chip.

REMEMBER THE MEMORY ➤ *pp. 10-11*
Random Access Memory (RAM) is vital to good PC performance.
To run Windows 95 efficiently, you'll need at least 8 megabytes of
RAM, and many PCs now come with 16 megabytes. You can add
extra memory any time, but it's pricey.

THINK BIG, TOO ➤ *pp. 11-12*
Today's software gobbles up storage space, so you should have a
hard disk drive with a capacity of at least 500 megabytes. That's no
problem if you're buying a new PC, because hard disks capable of
holding at least 1 gigabyte of information—that's 1,000 megabytes—
are common in systems being sold today.

SOUND OFF ➤ *pp. 13-17*

The future is here, and it's called *multimedia*. To take advantage of the cornucopia of sound, animation, and full-motion video now available, you'll need a CD-ROM drive, a stereo sound card and a pair of speakers. You'll also need a modem so you can tap into online services and the Internet.

SHOP SMART ➤ *pp. 18-21*

For under $2,000, you can get a fully loaded multimedia PC. But price isn't everything! Make sure you get the best possible deal, which includes strong service and technical support. And consider buying directly over the phone. If you deal with an established company, there's little risk, and it can save you hundreds of dollars.

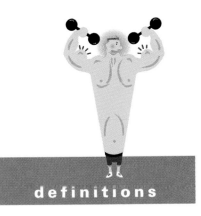

hardware: The electronic equipment that makes up a PC system.

software: Instructions that tell the PC what to do. As a rule of thumb, anything you plug in is hardware. Anything you can store on a disk is software.

In the span of a single generation, the personal computer has gone from science fiction concept to commodity item. Once the purview of those obsessed with technology (often referred to as geeks or nerds), PCs today are sold alongside televisions, stereo equipment, and other home appliances, and they've become indispensable tools in the workplace. The novelty has worn off, and folks are no longer dazzled by what a small humming box on a desktop can do. Busy people just want results. Fortunately, standards have developed in the past few years—for both hardware and software—that make using a PC a lot easier than it's ever been.

FROM USER-HOSTILE TO USER-FRIENDLY

When PCs first came out back in the early 1980s, using them was like chewing on nails. When you booted up your PC (and *boot* means *start* in this case, not *kick*), you'd be greeted by a dark, blank screen with a

```
C:\>
```

in the upper-left corner. That's called a *DOS* or *C prompt*. DOS, which stands for *D*isk *O*perating *S*ystem, was the basic underlying software of PCs until Windows showed up. To get anything done, you had to know DOS commands, which had to be typed in perfect order for them to work. For instance, to copy a file onto a floppy disk you might have entered this:

```
copy c:\dos\book.txt a:\dos\book.txt
```

What a pain!

"Would you realize what revolution is, call it Progress; and would you realize what progress is, call it Tomorrow."
—Victor Hugo

"Progress is man's ability to complicate simplicity."
—Thor Heyerdahl

definitions

click: To press the left mouse button once.

double-click: To press it twice in rapid succession.

right-click: To press the right mouse button once.

Throughout this book you'll see actions that involve clicking the buttons on your mouse or other pointing device.

Windows to the Rescue

Windows did away with the headache of DOS by providing a *graphical user interface* (or GUI—pronounced "gooey"). The blank screen with the DOS prompt was replaced by a virtual desktop featuring *icons*—little images you click to start programs. To illustrate how far technology has come, take a look Figure 1.1, which shows a "theme" desktop available for Windows 95.

Getting Around

Throughout this book, you'll find suggestions for using Windows 95 and other software to find out about your PC, customize it to your liking, and work in the most efficient way possible. In most cases, you'll start with the Start button, shown here,

which is located at the lower-left corner of the Windows 95 screen. Click it once to display the Start menu.

Figure 1.1 A wild screen display from Microsoft Plus! for Windows 95

While Windows has made life easier for PC users, it hasn't rid us of the jargon of the PC business. In fact, new terms continually pour into the marketplace as advances are made in both hardware and software. It's getting harder and harder to swim through the technology.

Tackling the Technobabble

Suppose you're in the market for a new PC. You certainly don't have to search very far. They're everywhere—in computer stores, home electronics stores, department stores, office stores, and even warehouse stores. But making an informed decision isn't so easy. A typical ad for a multimedia home PC might boast the following features:

- Pentium 100MHz processor
- 8MB of RAM, expandable to 128MB
- 1.2GB hard drive
- 4× CD-ROM drive
- PCI video with 1MB memory
- 15", 0.28 dot pitch color monitor
- 16-bit sound card
- 28.8 kbps fax modem

Yikes! If you're like most people, the only term that's going to have any meaning in this situation is MEGO, which stands for "My Eyes Glaze Over." Think about it. What other consumer product is so hard to understand? It makes programming your VCR look easy by comparison. Still, knowing what some of these acronyms and numbers mean can help you get the most PC for your money. The following rundown will help you cut through the technobabble.

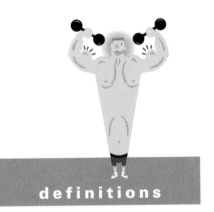

definitions

bit: *The smallest unit of information in computing.*

byte: *Eight bits, roughly equivalent to a character in the alphabet.*

kilobit (Kb): *1,000 bits.*

kilobyte (K or KB): *1,000 bytes.*

megabyte (MB): *Just over a million bytes—equal to about 500 pages of text.*

gigabyte (GB): *1,000 megabytes.*

THE MICROPROCESSOR

Let's take it from the top. The *microprocessor*—also known as the *central processing unit* (CPU) or the *chip*—is the most important part of the PC. The Pentium, made by Intel Corporation, is the fifth generation of chips designed specifically for PCs. Prior generations were known by numbers—286, 386, and 486 being the last three. Intel chose the name "Pentium" to get away from the numbering system that also was being used by its competitors. (A name could be trademarked; a number couldn't.)

The Main Brain

Although every PC has many other chips as well, the microprocessor is the brains of the outfit, controlling the flow of data throughout the system. Because that's the case, the PC is only as fast as its main chip. A Pentium encases 3.3 million transistors in a die about the size of a dime, as you can see here:

The Numbers Game

The performance of a microprocessor is rated by *clock speed,* which is measured in megahertz (MHz). A *megahertz* is equal to one million electrical vibrations per second. If the term seems familiar, it's because FM radio stations also transmit using megahertz frequencies. Over the years, refinements and advances in manufacturing have brought about chips that are smaller, less expensive—and much, much faster. The 486 chip started at 25MHz, and can now exceed 100. Pentiums range in speed from 75MHz to more than 150MHz, and by 1997, Intel expects to have chips with clock speeds of 300MHz.

How Fast Is Fast Enough?

If all you plan to do is word processing and surfing the Internet, a 486 chip should be just fine. If, on the other hand, you want to get into desktop publishing, or your kid likes to play 3-D video games on the PC, you'd better take the high road and go for a Pentium, which can manipulate graphics faster and run video smoother than older chips.

CAUTION

Be aware that the speeds of different kinds of chips are not directly comparable. For example, a 100MHz Pentium far outperforms a 100MHz 486. Speed figures are useful only for comparing chips of the same class.

When you turn off your PC,

everything stored in RAM is lost.

So make sure you save your

work to a disk first...otherwise,

heartache.

h a b i t s &
s t r a t e g i e s

Adding RAM may cost up to $50

per megabyte, so it's smart to

get the most memory possible at

the time you buy your system.

It's cheaper that way.

RAM

After the microprocessor, arguably the next most important feature of the PC is *RAM*. Shorthand for *Random Access Memory*, this is where computers temporarily store information while they're running. Think of RAM as an electronic version of your office desk, where you put your papers, pencils and coffee cup during the work day. RAM is measured in megabytes, and is built into finger-length modules containing chips that go inside the PC. To find out how much RAM your system has:

1. Choose Settings from the Start menu.
2. Select Control Panel.
3. Double-click on System to display the following dialog box:

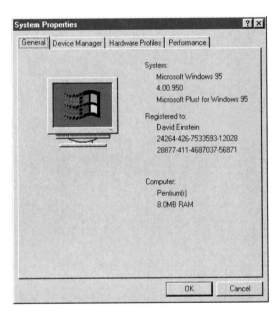

What You Really Need

To run Windows 95 effectively, you need at least 8MB of RAM, and 16 is even better. Multimedia applications, especially those with full-motion video, gobble up memory. Even a sophisticated word processing program will run much faster with 8 megs than with 4. And if you plan to do *multitasking*—that is, running more than one program at the same time—you'll need lots of memory. You can expand memory by adding more RAM chips. If you're buying a PC, make sure you can increase its memory to at least 32MB.

DISKS (AND DISCS)

To permanently store software programs as well as documents you create, the PC uses magnetic disks. These include hard disks, floppy disks, and compact discs called CD-ROMS. Floppies and CD-ROMs fit into openings at the front of your PC. Hard disks are entirely inside the PC console. The mechanisms that hold the disks are called drives, because they "drive" the disks by spinning them.

Hard Disk

A hard drive, like the one shown in Figure 1.2, can contain several circular platters, which collectively are referred to as the *hard disk*. These platters rotate very quickly, and information on them is read by

Figure 1.2 Cutaway of a hard disk drive

special heads, which also can "write" data onto the disk. Although you can't see the hard drive, there is a little green or yellow light on the front of your PC that indicates when the drive is in use.

Over the years, the capacity of hard disks has grown tremendously. In the late 1980s, a 20 or 40MB disk was considered satisfactory. Today, some PC disks can hold more than 2,000 megabytes.

The Bigger the Better

Do you need that much space? Probably not right now, but if history is any indication, you will at some point. Windows 95 alone can take up 60MB of room, while software applications and utilities can add hundreds more. At a minimum, don't settle for less than 500MB of storage capacity. And you shouldn't have to. PCs being sold today for around $2,000 routinely have hard disks capable of holding at least 1 gigabyte of information. (That's 1,000 megabytes or a billion bytes, whichever sounds more impressive.)

Floppy Disks

The 3½ inch diameter *floppy disk* fits into an opening in the front of the PC, and is used primarily to load software onto the hard disk. Like a hard disk, a floppy is a magnetically treated disk on which digitized information can be stored. At first glance, the disk may not seem floppy, but inside the hard plastic shell there really is a thin, flexible disk. (Trust me on this one. If you break open the disk, you'll ruin it.)

A Little History on Floppies

The first floppies were 8 inches in diameter, and really floppy. By the 1980s, floppies were down to 5¼ inches, and now the 3½-inch disk has taken over. It's still thin and bendable, but it's protected by a hard plastic cover, so it doesn't appear floppy at all. The disks used today have a capacity of 1.44MB of data, twice what the first 3½-inch floppies could hold. If you have any of these older 3½-inchers lying around, don't fret. They'll work fine in a high-capacity drive.

Before you can use a floppy disk, it must be formatted. Formatting imprints the operating system onto the disk so that the PC can recognize it. You can buy disks pre-formatted, or format them yourself.

CAUTION

Formatting a disk erases everything on it. So make sure the new floppy you're formatting is really new, and not one that's been lying around with old files on it that you're going to want some day.

FORMATTING A FLOPPY DISK step by step

1. Put a new, unformatted disk into the floppy drive.
2. Double-click on the My Computer icon at the upper left corner of the Windows 95 desktop.
3. Right-click on the icon titled ½ Floppy (A:).
4. Choose Format, which gives you the screen you see here.
5. Select the options you want, and click Start to begin formatting your floppy.

```
Format - 3½ Floppy (A:)                    [?] [X]

Capacity:
[1.44 Mb (3.5")                      ▼]      Start

┌─ Format type ─────────────────┐           Close
│  ○ Quick (erase)              │
│  ○ Full                       │
│  ○ Copy system files only     │
└───────────────────────────────┘

┌─ Other options ───────────────┐
│  Label:                       │
│  [                         ]  │
│                               │
│  ☐ No label                   │
│  ☑ Display summary when finished │
│  ☐ Copy system files          │
└───────────────────────────────┘

[                               ]
```

MULTIMEDIA

The biggest step forward in PCs in the 1990s has been the addition of *multimedia*—animated graphics, sound, and video. In fact, multimedia has been the driving force behind PC sales since 1994. To participate in this brave new world of sight and sound, you need a CD-ROM drive, a sound card, and a pair of stereo speakers. Fortunately, all new home PCs come with the necessary gear. It's also possible, and fairly painless, to add multimedia capabilities to an existing PC. You'll learn how to do that in Chapter 3.

CD-ROM

This acronym stands for *C*ompact *D*isc-*R*ead *O*nly *M*emory. It's the same format as an audio CD, and in fact, you can play music CDs on your PC if you have a set of speakers attached. In addition to sound, CD-ROMs feature graphics, animation, photos, and even full-motion video, like the movie scene you see in Figure 1.3. A CD-ROM can hold a lot of information—more than 650MB. But there is a disadvantage: You can't store data on them. That's what the "Read Only" part means.

When referring to hard and floppy disks, the word disk is spelled with a k. For CDs, it ends with a c. The first CDs were only for music, and had nothing to do with computers. It's only been in the last few years that the format has been used for encyclopedias, games, etc.

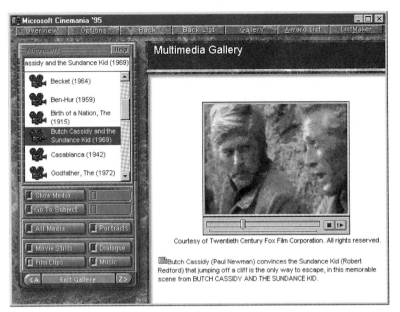

Figure 1.3 A video clip from *Butch Cassidy and the Sundance Kid* on Microsoft Cinemania '95. There's even sound…"Kid, the next time I say let's go someplace like Bolivia, let's GO someplace like Bolivia!"

Actually, the technology that will let you store data on a CD is already here—now it's just a question of getting the price down so real folks can afford it.

Gaining Speed

CD-ROMs are quite slow compared to hard disks, but they're getting faster. We've gone from single-speed to double-speed to quad-speed CD-ROM drives (referred to as 4× drives, which now are the norm), and it's only a question of time before 6× and 8× models become common. Most CD-ROM drives feature trays like those in audio CD players. A few models make you put the CD-ROM into a removable caddy that fits into the opening in the drive. Faster CD-ROM drives improve video quality and the speed or action in video games. You need at least a 2× drive for smooth animation and video.

Sound

A multimedia PC processes audio through a *sound card* mounted inside the computer. For CD-quality stereo, you need a 16-bit sound

Besides multimedia, CD-ROMs increasingly are being used for packaging big software programs. This can make life a lot easier. For instance, Windows 95 takes up more than a dozen floppies, but only one CD.

card. PC makers usually include special software that lets you use the sound card to record voice and music, customize the sound, and even use your CD-ROM drive as you would an audio CD player. (See Figure 1.4.)

Video

One of the most overlooked features of the PC (pun intended) is its video capability. All Windows-compatible PCs can display graphics, but the speed and quality of video can vary greatly. This is one area that it pays to ask about, just to make sure you're getting the latest technology. The emerging standard for video works with what is called PCI, or *P*eripheral *C*omponent *I*nterconnect—a method of linking components within the computer to make everything work faster. You'll get a full explanation in Chapter 3. For shopping purposes, just remember to look for the PCI designation.

Monitor

Most PCs sold for the home include a *monitor,* also called the *display* or *screen.* A PC monitor uses a cathode ray tube, like a

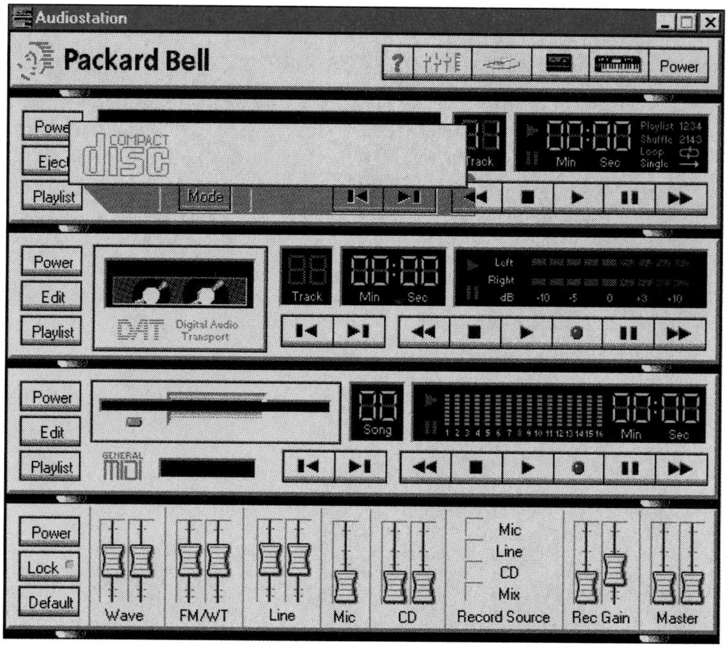

Figure 1.4 This PC audiostation looks a lot like a home stereo.

television, but that's where the comparison ends. Monitors have to create a crisp, clear display of small text, while TVs are made to show moving images. A PC monitor is far more expensive than a TV with the same size screen, because it has to be able to clearly display still images, including the small text. It's that high cost that keeps monitor sizes down. The average monitor used on today's home PC is 15 inches measured diagonally. Small though it is, a good monitor is capable of amazing clarity and color, as you can see in Figure 1.5

Picture Quality

You're not getting tired of technical terms yet, are you? Well, here's another one—*dot pitch*. It refers to the distance between tiny dots that together form pictures on a monitor. The smaller the distance, the clearer the picture. A dot pitch of 0.28 millimeters is considered good for a 15-inch monitor. Some PC makers try to fob off monitors with dot pitches as high as 0.39 mm, which can make it hard to work with complex graphics or small text.

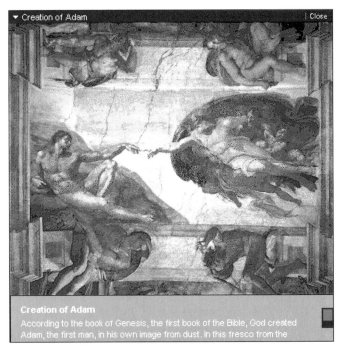

Figure 1.5 A section of the ceiling of the Sistine Chapel painted by Michelangelo, as depicted in Microsoft Encarta

Modem

To hook up to the Internet, a commercial online service or your company's office network, you'll need a *modem,* which converts data and transmits it through telephone lines. Modems can be either internal circuit cards, or external devices that plug into the back of the PC. Internal modems are cheaper, but they're harder to install. Virtually all new home PCs come with internal modems.

Speed Is Key

The speed of a modem is measured in how many bits of data it can send per second (bps). The industry is now moving toward a standard speed of 28.8 kbps (kilobits per second), up from 14.4 kbps just a year ago. Here's a quick, easy way to find out what kind of modem you have:

1. Choose Settings from the Start menu.
2. Click on Control Panel.
3. Double-click on the Modems folder to get the information you're looking for. You'll see a screen that looks much like this one:

definition

baud: *Sometimes used interchangeably with* bps *to define the speed of a modem. That's wrong. Technically,* baud *refers to changes in a communications signal, not the amount of data that can travel through the line. Also, not to be confused with* Bard, *which was Shakespeare.*

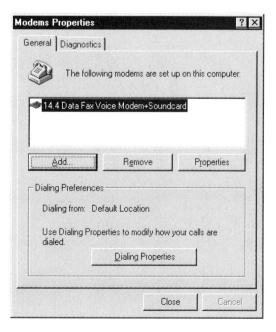

ADDING IT ALL UP

If you're considering buying a new PC, prepare to pay between $1,500 and $2,000 for a system with everything on the list that started this chapter. PCs using older 486 chips, with smaller hard drives and monitors and slower modems, can be had for under $1,500. High-power systems, for computer-aided engineering and other complex programs, can run well over $3,000. How much PC you need will depend on how you plan to use it. If your needs are light, that two- or three-year-old PC you already have could be enough. Here are a few examples of systems suited to certain tasks:

	Word Processing or Spreadsheets	Multimedia and Games	Graphics, Publishing, or Engineering
Microprocessor:	486DX-33	Pentium 90	Pentium 133
RAM:	8MB	8 to 16MB	16 to 32MB
Hard Drive:	540MB	850MB	1.6GB
Monitor:	14"	15"	17" or 21"
Video Memory:	1MB	1MB	2MB

The Notebook Alternative

If you need to use a PC when you travel, or if space is at a premium in your home, a *notebook* PC may be just the ticket. Notebooks—which used to be called *laptops*—weigh under ten pounds, fit in a briefcase, and in many cases can be as powerful as desktop systems. In fact, a high-end notebook can even include a CD-ROM.

Beware the Drawbacks

The convenience of small size carries a big price. Feature-for-feature, notebook PCs cost far more than full-size systems. Also, add-ons such as modems cost more for notebooks. And their batteries typically must be recharged after several hours, which limits the time you'll be able to use your notebook away from an electrical source.

habits & strategies

With PC technology advancing so rapidly, it pays to look ahead when you shop. If you spend a little more for a system with a fast chip and a big hard drive, you'll sleep better knowing that it will still be considered a robust PC next year.

HOW TO BUY A PC

The two primary ways to purchase a PC are in a retail store and by direct mail. Both have advantages. If you go to a store, you can try out the machine, and you don't have to wait for it to come in the mail. This is the way most people buy PCs. In recent years, however, direct sales have garnered a following. Several major PC makers sell ONLY over the phone. The benefits of buying direct are that you pay less for a comparable system sold in a store, and you can usually customize the system with the components you want.

Room to Grow

Even though today's PCs all have more or less the same specifications, there are some significant differences you should be aware of. For instance, some PCs provide more room than others for expansion—adding a new modem, sound card, or disk drive, for instance. Your PC should come with at least three available expansion slots for internal plug-in cards, plus at least one empty drive bay. You can see how many expansion slots there are simply by looking at the back of your PC, as shown here:

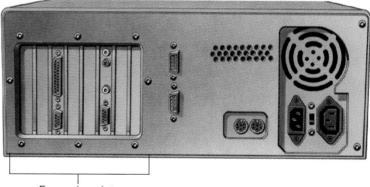

Expansion slots

Software Bundles

Most PC makers offer extensive software bundles that can include top-flight productivity programs, as well as CD-ROM encyclopedias, games, and personal finance software (shown in Figure 1.6). One company was recently offering 40 software titles in its bundle.

Figure 1.6 Intuit's Quicken personal finance software is bundled with many PCs.

out-of-box experience: A term

cooked up by PC makers. In a

good out-of-box experience, the

system is easy to set up, with

pre-loaded software that lets

you start using your new PC right

away. By comparison, early PCs

came with no software, and just

sat around till you got some.

The idea is to give the user a nice out-of-box experience. That's admirable, but usually most of the software that's included is second-tier stuff that will be used little, if at all. In the final analysis, the out-of-box experience is less important than the out-of-pocket experience. Thus, the main considerations when buying a new PC should be price, reliability, technical support, and service.

Product Support

Because a PC is a big investment, you're going to want to buy from a company that backs up its products. Look for the following:

- At least a three-year warranty on hardware. That's the norm for many big PC makers these days, but there are others that offer only stingy one-year warranties.
- A PC maker who's been in business for awhile and is strong financially. A well-established company is more likely to be around for the life of the warranty.

A word about manuals: Traditionally, PC and software instruction manuals have been nearly as difficult to decipher as the Rosetta Stone. These days many PC makers are reducing the size of paper manuals and putting more documentation on CDs. Good move. It saves them money, and saves you a lot of frustration. But don't worry if you don't get a thick manual with your PC. You can proceed without fear, having wisely bought this book.

- A 30-day, money-back guarantee—either from the PC maker or the retailer. And check to see whether the manufacturer provides on-site service, a big plus if your PC is essential to your business.
- Good telephone support for technical problems. Some manufacturers offer sterling support, others drop the ball and make you suffer through lengthy waits on the phone. Leading computer magazines routinely do surveys that can clue you as to which companies take the best care of their customers.

CONGRATULATIONS!

You've passed "Personal Computer Jargon 101." Now it's time to discuss some of the things that attach to the computer, like the keyboard, the mouse, some more stuff about the monitor, and the printer—devices that let you enter information into the PC, and then let you see the results of your handiwork.

Putting It All Together

FAST FORWARD

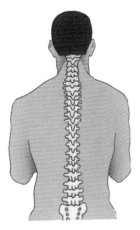

THINK HEALTHY ➤ *pp. 26-27*

Set up your PC with ergonomics in mind. Use an adjustable chair, if possible, and keep the PC out of direct light. And sit up straight like your mother told you to!

STAY IN CONTROL ➤ *pp. 29-30*

Many of the basic adjustments for PC equipment can be done through the Windows 95 Control Panel. To reach it:

1. Choose Settings from the Start menu.
2. Click Control Panel.

IMPROVE THE PICTURE ➤ *pp. 30-35*

If you have a Super VGA monitor—and most PCs sold in the last few years do—set it to give you 800×600 resolution and 256 colors. This will let you take full advantage of Windows software and give you the clearest possible display.

DON'T BE TYPECAST ➤ *pp. 35-39*

Keyboards differ widely in how they feel when you type on them. Here, for instance, you see an ergonomically enhanced model from Kinesis. If you don't like the response your keyboard gives you, don't be bashful about swapping it for another one. PC keyboards are pretty inexpensive, and easy to install.

MASTER THAT MOUSE ➤ *pp. 40-41*

If you're using Windows 95 and the software that works with it, the right button on your mouse finally has a major role to play. Right-clicking brings up small menus that let you perform basic operations such as copying, cutting and pasting.

PICK OUT A PRINTER ➤ *pp. 42-45*

There are three main types of PC printers you can choose from: *Dot matrix* printers are fast and loud, and their print quality is nothing fancy; they're suitable for generating high-volume data printouts. *Laser* printers give you excellent quality and use regular typing paper, but they're rather slow and expensive—especially the ones that print in color. *Inkjet* printers approach the type quality of laser printers, but they're not as expensive; color inkjets are currently quite popular.

Once you've purchased your printer, you must install a software driver on your system for the brand and model you've selected:

1. From the Start menu, choose Settings.
2. Click Printers.
3. Double-click the Add Printer icon. This takes you to the Add Printer Wizard, a Windows feature that guides you through the installation process.

Your PC is a collection of components—the PC console itself, the monitor, the keyboard, the printer, and so on—that work together as a system. In this chapter you'll learn the basics of setting up your system, as well as how to configure each major piece of equipment to deliver the best performance. The most important thing to remember is not to be afraid of fooling around with adjustments and controls. Go ahead, experiment. You can't hurt the equipment, and you just might discover something that makes your computing life easier.

SETTING UP YOUR PC

The PC isn't just for work anymore. It's also an entertainment console, a place to conduct family finances, and a study center. With this in mind, it's best to set up your PC so that everyone in your family can benefit from it. Of course, if one household member will be using the system a lot more than anyone else, set it up primarily for that person.

Sitting Pretty

You can avoid PC-related injuries, sometimes called *RSI*, by setting up your work area wisely. Think of the PC as a piano, and think of yourself as a classical pianist—back straight, wrists straight, forearms parallel to the floor. As a rule of thumb, your keyboard should be at the same height as your elbows. You can usually achieve perfect computing posture using a chair whose height and back can be adjusted. While seated, your eyes should be level with the top of the viewing area on your monitor. That way, you'll be looking slightly downward, which is a good, comfortable angle. The monitor should be tilted so that you face it straight-on. Figure 2.1 shows a well-configured work area.

definition

RSI: Repetitive Stress Injury. *A collective label for any disability caused by repeating a physical movement over and over. Typing for long periods at a PC can cause RSI injuries to the hands, wrists, elbows, arms and back.*

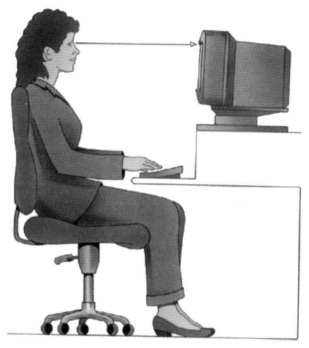

Figure 2.1 An ergonomically sound work area

A Well-Lighted Place

If you've ever tried to watch a television near a bright window, you know the problems direct light can cause. The same holds for PCs. Avoid placing the computer near a window, unless you can reduce the light with drapes or shutters. Bright artificial light also can make it hard to see things on the monitor—especially light coming from directly in front of or behind the monitor. Side-lighting is preferable, and reflected lighting is best.

Glare Shields and Hoods

If lighting is a problem that can't be fixed, consider getting a glare shield. This is a piece of special glass or plastic that fits over your screen. Another option is a plastic hood that goes on the monitor and provides an overhang on the top and sides, preventing too much light from reaching the screen.

Powering Up

Assuming you have a typical multimedia PC system, it's going to require at least four electrical outlets—one each for the PC, monitor, printer and stereo speakers. Since you're likely to have only one wall outlet in the immediate vicinity, you should get a power strip with four or six outlets on it. Power strips are available at hardware stores, electronics stores and such.

Power Protection

Power outages or sudden changes in electrical currents can damage your PC and destroy your data. There are ways to guard against power losses, however. A surge suppressor will protect your system from glitches in the electricity. Many power strips include surge suppressors, but these are usually only modestly effective. For the best protection, get a dedicated surge suppressor. And if your electric company is really unreliable, consider an uninterruptable power supply (UPS), a device that continues to run your PC on battery power for a short time in the event of an electrical outage.

Getting Connected

Monitors, printers, keyboards, and mice connect to the back of the PC. The shapes and sizes of the connectors have become standardized over time. On many newer PCs, connections are either color-coded or distinctly labeled to help you hook everything up.

Different Kinds of Connections

Sooner or later you're probably going to run into terms like "parallel port" and "serial port." Basically, a *port* is an interface between the PC and some piece of equipment, such as a printer or modem. The only reason you'd want to know that you have a *parallel port* is because that's

where the printer connects, so you need one. Similarly, if you have two *serial ports,* you can connect both a mouse and an external modem. FYI, here's what a few of the terms mean:

- **Parallel port** A connection that allows data to flow along high-speed parallel lines. Used mostly for printers.
- **Serial port** A connection through which bits of data are sent, one after another. Used for mice, modems, and other peripherals.
- **PS/2 port** Also called a *mouse port,* this connects a mouse to the PC, freeing up a serial port for something else. Note that a PS/2 port will resemble the port where you plug in your keyboard—but the two are not interchangeable! PS/2 ports are becoming more popular, but lots of PCs still rely on serial ports for mice.

Here's how some common PC connections are shaped:

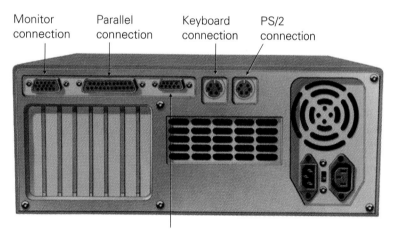

Serial connection

BASIC HARDWARE

The different parts of your PC system appear easy enough to operate. They all have fewer controls than a stereo receiver. Yet monitors, printers, and other devices can be quite sophisticated. It's worth getting to know them individually so that you can use them as effectively as possible with Windows 95 and other software.

Your Hardware Control Center

In order to customize the way hardware works with the rest of your system, you'll almost always go through the Control Panel in Windows 95. To get there, choose Settings from the Start menu, and then click Control Panel. As you can see here, the Control Panel is a collection of icons representing major parts of your PC system.

MONITORS

Anyone who stares at a video display for eight hours a day knows how important a good monitor is. But even a first-class monitor must be adjusted to bring out the best possible picture. To do this, you work with the controls on the monitor itself, as well as others available through Windows.

Tweaking the Knobs

In most cases, your monitor will have at least two adjustable knobs on the front. One is the *brightness* control, which, as the term implies, controls the brightness of the images on the screen. The other, the *contrast* knob, adjusts the difference between the lightest and darkest areas of the display. These knobs can help compensate for difficult lighting situations. How you adjust them is strictly a matter of taste.

Other Screen Controls

Depending on the quality of your monitor, it may have other adjustable controls as well. Common ones include vertical and horizontal positioning for centering the image on the screen, as well as controls that let you adjust the maximum size of the viewing area. In older monitors, the controls are usually knobs. In new ones, they are buttons that allow digital onscreen adjustments.

CONFIGURING A MONITOR step by step

Suppose you outgrow your old 14-inch monitor and splurge on a new 15- or 17-inch model. Here's how to set up Windows to work with your new beauty.

1. From the Control Panel, choose Display.

2. Select the Settings tab.

3. Click Change Display Type.

4. Click Change Button For Monitor Type. The Select Device screen will appear.

5. If your monitor came with installation software, click the Have Disk button and follow the instructions.

6. If you don't have special software, try to find your monitor on the

Select Device

Click the Monitor that matches your hardware, and then click OK. If you don't know which model you have, click OK. If you have an installation disk for this device, click Have Disk.

Manufacturers:
- (Standard monitor types)
- Aamazing Technologies
- Acer
- Actix Systems, Inc.
- Adara Technology, Inc.

Models:
- Plug and Play Monitor (VESA DDC)
- Standard VGA 640x480
- Super VGA 800x600
- Super VGA 1024x768
- Super VGA 1280x1024
- Super VGA 1600x1200

○ Show compatible devices
● Show all devices

Have Disk...

OK   Cancel

Making It Perfectly Clear

The single biggest factor affecting picture quality is *resolution*, which refers to the number of *pixels* that can be displayed on the screen. To work with Windows, you need a *VGA* monitor capable of displaying 640×480 resolution. A Super VGA monitor can display 800×600. Larger monitors can handle even higher resolutions, such as 1024×768 or even 1280×1024, which are needed for intricate design work and graphics.

definitions

VGA: Video Graphics Array.
A standard for PC monitors that superseded previous standards such as CGA and EGA (since they're all out of date, you don't need definitions of them).

pixel: *Stands for* picture element. *A cluster of three colored dots (red, blue and green). Pixels combine to form images on your PC screen.*

Refresh Rate

This is what determines how steady the picture is on your screen. The *refresh rate* refers to how frequently the monitor redraws the entire display from top to bottom. It's measured in hertz, and 72Hz is considered acceptable for high resolutions. At that rate the screen won't flicker, which your eyes will be thankful for.

Better but Smaller

Higher resolutions are nice, but they have their drawbacks, the major one being that as resolution increases, the size of the picture decreases. Here, the screen on the top is set at 640×480, while the bottom one is set at 1024×768:

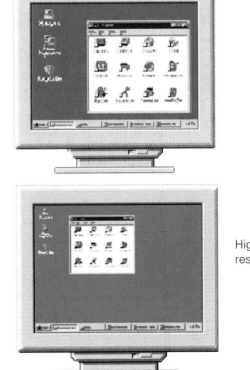

Lower resolution

Higher resolution

If your monitor features size-adjustment controls, you can enlarge higher-resolution images to better fill the screen.

driver: *A software file containing information the PC needs to operate a monitor, printer, or other peripheral device. Many devices come with their own drivers, but Windows also supplies drivers for many popular brands.*

A World of Color

Inside the PC is a chip or circuit card that determines how many colors can be displayed. The lowest number usually is 16, the highest 16.7 million. Are there really that many colors? No. Why does the PC industry think there are? Your guess is as good as mine. For today's multimedia software, the standard setting is 256 colors, which is more than comes in a box of crayons.

Making the Adjustments

Some PCs are configured at the factory with a *video driver* set for 640×480 resolution and just 16 colors, but you can use Windows to change these settings. First, however, check your instruction manuals to see how much color and resolution your system can handle. To make changes, go to the Control Panel and double-click Display. Then choose the Settings tab, which will bring up the *dialog box* you see here:

Display Properties

Background | Screen Saver | Appearance | Plus! | Settings

Color palette
256 Color

Desktop area
Less ——|—— More
800 by 600 pixels

Font size
Small Fonts   Custom...

Change Display Type...

OK   Cancel   Apply

CAUTION

If you're running out of room on your hard disk, you might think twice before installing a screen saver that features complex animation or full-motion video. Those puppies can take up a lot of storage space.

To change the resolution, slide the gauge for the Desktop area. To increase the number of colors, click the arrow box in the Color palette section and make a new choice.

Screen Savers

If you're going to leave your system on and unattended for long periods of time, consider using a screen saver. By keeping the display in motion, screen savers prevent images from "burning in" and leaving ghosts on the screen. (There is some differing of opinion as to whether screen savers actually work, but some of them sure look good.) Dozens of screen saver programs are available commercially, featuring everything from cartoon themes to scenes from popular TV shows.

Windows Screen Savers If all you're looking for is a basic screen saver, you don't have to buy anything, because Windows 95 comes with several screen savers built in. To activate one of them, go to the Control Panel and choose Display. Then pick the Screen Saver tab to bring up the following dialog box:

Display Properties	? X

Background | **Screen Saver** | Appearance | Plus! | Settings

Screen Saver

Flying Windows   Settings...   Preview

☐ Password protected   Change...   Wait: 3 minutes

Energy saving features of monitor

☐ Low-power standby 4 minutes

☐ Shut off monitor 4 minutes

OK   Cancel   Apply

From here you can choose the screen saver you want and decide how fast the action will be and how long the PC must remain unused before the screen saver kicks in.

Notebook Monitors

Don't expect as much out of a notebook screen as you get with a desktop monitor. For one thing, they aren't as big. The average notebook screen measures less than 11 inches (diagonally). And notebook screens typically have 640×480 resolution—the low end of what you can get out of a desktop monitor. Nonetheless, notebook screens have come a long way. Most of them are now color, whereas just a few years ago most were black-and-white. There are two basic types of color screens for notebooks:

- **Active matrix** In an active matrix display, each pixel on the screen has its own transistor. This is the clearest—and most expensive—kind of color for notebooks. It also consumes power fastest, which can be tough on a notebook's battery.
- **Passive matrix** In this display, there's one transistor for every column or row. Most passive matrix screens are *dual-scan,* which means they offer twice the contrast of single-scan screens.

THE KEYBOARD

It's an irony of the PC age that, despite all our technological advances, we're still tethered to a keyboard. Basically, it's a glorified version of the same keyboard that graced the typewriter for more than a century before the PC came along. So far, nobody's come up with an alternative that's been able to catch on. Old habits, it seems, die hard, even in the computer age.

101 Keys

Today's standard PC keyboard has 101 keys. But don't worry, you probably will never have occasion to use a lot of them. The average person spends the most time typing happily in the main body of keys, which looks more or less like a traditional typewriter keyboard. Besides the main typing area, there are several other groups of keys, as shown in Figure 2.2. They include:

Most notebooks have connectors for external monitors. This allows you to hook up your notebook to a full-size monitor for Super VGA display, or even to a projector for presentations.

- A number pad that lets you input numbers using just one hand. Whoopie!
- Arrows for moving the cursor around in a document (good also as direction keys in some games).
- A block of keys including PAGE UP, PAGE DOWN, HOME and END, which let you move quickly through a document or back to the beginning.
- Function keys—usually 12 of them.

Function keys   Number pad

Cursor keys

Figure 2.2 A standard 101-key PC keyboard

Good Keys to Know

There are a few keys that can save you time and get you out of tough jams. Here's a rundown of the most important:

ENTER This is the key that gets things done. It completes commands, telling the PC it's okay to open, close, save, print, etc. If an onscreen button has a dark border around it, you can hit ENTER to choose it, instead of clicking on the button with your mouse. In word processing, the ENTER key acts like a RETURN key on an electric typewriter, starting a new paragraph.

CTRL At the lower corners of the main group of keys are two identical keys marked CTRL (for *Control*). While it may seem odd to have two CTRL keys, they actually can make it easier to enter key combinations. Most software lets you use a CTRL key in combination with other keys to issue commands, which can be quicker than using a mouse or other pointing device. For instance, you usually can save a file simply by pressing the CTRL and S keys at the same time (CTRL-S). You'll learn more of these shortcuts in Chapter 4.

ESC This is the Escape key, which, as the name implies, causes most programs to stop what they're doing. For instance, you can often stop multimedia programs, such as games and videos, by pressing ESC.

INSERT This key toggles between Insert and Overstrike modes. In Insert mode, you can insert text within a paragraph. In Overstrike mode, you simply type over what's already there.

The F Keys

On most keyboards the function keys, labeled F1 through F12, are lined up across the top. Ironically, these keys have very little function for the average PC user. This wasn't always the case. In the years before the mouse came into vogue, you needed those function keys to operate the computer. Alone or in conjunction with the CTRL or ALT keys, they let you create, open, close, save and print documents, as well as perform every other operation. Today, function keys are used in a lot of business software for corporate networks. They also are incorporated into consumer programs and can provide handy shortcuts that let you bypass menus. (In Microsoft Word for Windows, for instance, pressing F7 launches the spell checker.) And let's not forget the ever-popular F1 key, which usually will call up the "help" screen for the application you're using.

More or Less Useless Keys

In some ways, the PC age has passed parts of the keyboard by. Just in case you're wondering, here's what some of the extra keys do (or don't do):

- **PRINT SCREEN/SYSRQ** If you're still working in DOS, this key will send whatever's on the screen to your printer. In Windows, it sends it to the clipboard, so you can copy it into another program. SYSRQ stands for *System Request*. It doesn't do anything, so forget it.
- **PAUSE/BREAK** Causes a scrolling screen in DOS to stop. Useless in Windows.
- **SCROLL LOCK** A toggle key that, in some applications, enables the direction keys to scroll the entire document instead of moving the cursor.

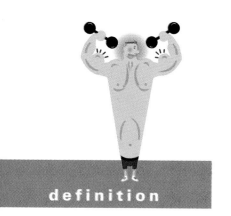

definition

CAPS LOCK: This is the computer version of the old SHIFT LOCK key on the typewriter. In the case of the PC, it capitalizes all letters, but does not "shift" special keys or the numbers row. This means you can easily type DX486/100, for instance, within Caps Lock mode.

Customizing the Keyboard

There's not a whole lot you can do vis à vis changing how your keyboard works. Double-click the Keyboard icon in the Control Panel to view your options:

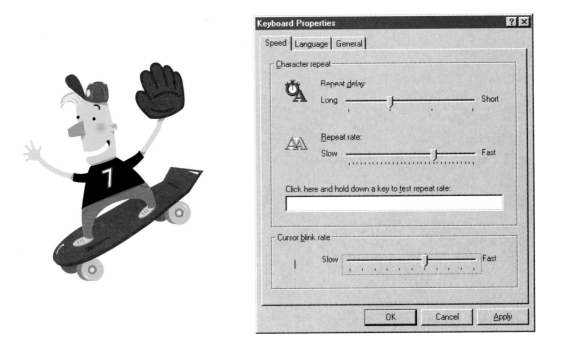

Basically you can change the speed at which keystrokes repeat if you hold a key down, and you can speed up or slow down the blinking of the cursor.

Look and Feel

Even though PC keyboards look almost identical these days, they don't "feel" identical. There are big differences in the way they respond. The amount of pressure it takes to type varies from one to the next, as does the actual sensation of the keys on the fingertips. Even the sound differs from keyboard to keyboard. Some are practically silent, while others tap like a typewriter. In short, a keyboard that's just right for one person may be all wrong for another.

Replacing Your Keyboard

Don't hesitate to get a new keyboard if the one that came with your PC is not to your liking. You can find replacement keyboards starting at less than $50 at computer and office stores. Some newer keyboards also have special keys for launching programs in Windows 95. To change keyboards, double-click the Keyboard icon in the Control Panel, select the General tab, click the Change button, and follow the instructions from there.

Ergonomic Keyboards

The realization that working nonstop at a PC can cause health problems has led to a new generation of *ergonomic* keyboards. These devices take some getting used to. Many of them "split" the keyboard in half, and angle the sections so your hands rest on the keys at a more natural angle. Little solid research has been done to ascertain whether this approach really helps, but the companies that make them claim it does. Ergonomic keyboards, such as the Microsoft model shown here, start at under $100.

Notebook Keyboards

Notebook keyboards take some getting used to if you ordinarily work on a standard PC. The keys on a notebook are usually smaller and packed in closer together, and there are fewer special keys. As a result, some keys have multiple functions. For instance, there may be an Fn key that you hold down while pressing a number key to produce the result of a function key. And to think notebooks were designed for busy people! Go figure.

INPUT DEVICES

Many of the basic operations of the PC, such as opening, closing and saving files, can be performed using a mouse or other input device. In fact, one of the joys of Windows is its ability to take advantage of the mouse, and free you from relying on hard-to-remember keyboard combinations to get things done.

Mouse Basics

Most mice come with two buttons; a few come with three. Windows 95 software takes advantage of both the left and right buttons. If there's a middle button, usually it can be customized to perform special duties. The left button is the main one; you make selections by pointing to stuff and clicking the left button, and you drag objects around by holding down the button while you move the mouse. The right button calls up short *context menus*, also called shortcut menus, that let you quickly perform common tasks appropriate to whatever you're working on. Say, for instance, you're writing a letter and want to move some text. Highlight the section you want to move and right-click the highlighted text. You'll see something like this:

Cut
Copy
Paste
Font...
Paragraph...
Bullets and Numbering...

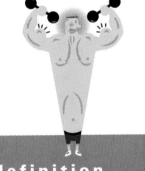

dialog box: a device that Windows uses to provide you with information about a procedure, and give you ways to handle it. Basically, anytime you're presented with options such as OK or Cancel, you're looking at a dialog box.

Click Cut. Then move the cursor to the spot where you want the type to go. Right-click again, click Paste, and you've done it.

Mice Can Learn

Windows 95 lets you tailor how your mouse works. You can reverse the operations of the left and right buttons (good deal for left-handers), and even control the sensitivity of the little creature. To fiddle with the mouse settings, click the Mouse icon in the Control Panel. If you're using Windows' own mouse driver, you'll see the following dialog box:

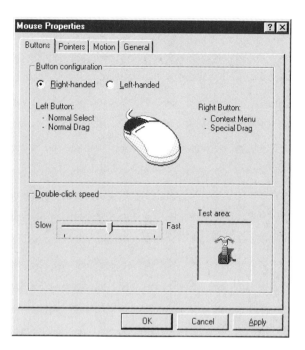

If your mouse came with another brand of driver and you're using it instead of the Windows driver, the box you see will look somewhat different.

One Last Thing...

Clean your mouse once in a while! First turn off the PC and unplug the mouse. Then remove the ball from the bottom and wipe off the dust. Use a cotton swab to clean out the ball casing. A clean mouse will operate more smoothly; be aware, however, that PC mice wear out and die, just like real mice.

Other Input Devices

Although the mouse is by far the most popular form of input device, there are alternatives for PC users who don't like to push a mouse around.

Trackballs

One option is the trackball, in which the ball is larger and located on top of the device instead of underneath—sort of an upside-down mouse, as you can see here. This design allows you to move the cursor by moving the ball directly; the device itself stays in one place.

Touch Pads

Touch pads are small rectangular pads that are pressure sensitive. You simply touch the pad with a finger and trace the path along which you want the cursor to travel. Some touch pads even allow you to select items by tapping (or double-tapping) on the pad itself.

Input Devices for Notebooks

Most notebook PCs come with a built-in pointing device. Some manufacturers use trackballs; others favor a rubberized pointer that sits in the middle of the keyboard. Touch pads also are starting to become popular. If you aren't comfortable with the input device on your notebook—and lots of people aren't—you can usually hook up a mouse. If this is your plan, your notebook needs to have a PS/2 mouse port or a serial port. Most notebooks come with one or the other, or both.

PRINTERS

One of the fastest growing segments of the PC industry is the printer business. Rapid advances in technology have given consumers a new generation of printers that enable us to produce professional-looking reports, brochures, newsletters—even books—right at home.

The Options

There are three main types of printers for PCs—*dot matrix, laser,* and *inkjet.* Each one has certain advantages, but the inkjet appears to

dpi: dots per inch. *A way of measuring print quality by counting how many dots a printer can fit in a linear inch. As with most PC definitions, it's useful mostly as a comparative measurement.*

Color or black-and-white? Assuming you go for an inkjet printer, you might as well opt for color. It'll cost you a little more, but with so many software applications now able to generate color, it can really help you take advantage of what your PC can do. And a colorful report or presentation might help a busy person win points at the office.

be gaining the most in popularity due to its combination of high-quality output and low cost.

Dot Matrix

Like typewriters, dot matrix printers work by impact. They generate type by striking little pins onto a ribbon. They're the fastest of all printers, but their print quality is the worst, and they can be noisy. Dot matrix printers are used mostly for high-volume printing of things like statistics.

Laser Printers

Laser printers work like copy machines to print pages one at a time. Great quality—up to 600 dpi in home models—but slow. They're the most expensive printers, and toner cartridges also are pricey. Laser printers that do color are really expensive.

Inkjets

Inkjets get their name from the way they work—by spraying ink from tiny jets to form letters and graphics on paper. Inkjet printers with resolutions of greater than 300 dpi start at about $200, and color models can be had for under $300, although fancy models are more expensive. Like laser printers, inkjets use regular typing paper. The ink is contained in replaceable cartridges. Type quality approaches that of lasers.

Adding a Printer

To add a printer to your system, you must install a software driver for the particular brand and model of printer. To do this, choose Settings from the Start menu, click Printers, and double-click the Add Printer icon. This will take you to a Wizard —a Windows feature that guides you through a procedure. Click the Next button, which brings up this window:

This is where you choose what kind of printer you want to add to your system. Windows 95 includes drivers for many popular printers. If you don't see your model on the list, you'll have to use the software that came with your printer to install it. Click the Have Disk button and go for it.

SETTING A DEFAULT PRINTER step by step

If you have more than one printer connected to your PC, or if you have fax software, you'll have to designate a default printer. (Fax programs act as virtual printers in Windows.) The default printer is the one your PC will use unless you specify otherwise. To set a default printer, do the following:

1 From the Start menu, choose Settings.

2. Click Printers (obviously).

3. Right-click the icon for the printer you want to bring up.

4. In the shortcut menu, click Set As Default.

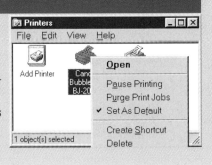

Ready to Print

In order to print, your printer must be *online*—in other words, ready to receive information from the PC. When you turn your printer on, it automatically goes through a setup routine to get into online mode. If it runs out of paper or ink, it takes itself off line. Very sensible, these printers! To put the printer back online after you replace the ink cartridge or the paper, press the Online button. There may also be other buttons, for cleaning the print head, positioning envelopes in the printer, and other procedures. Consult your manual for details.

Stopping the Printer

There are times when you'll want to stop printing in the middle of a document. Your printer may run out of ink, or you'll suddenly realize there's a mistake you have to fix. Don't panic. Just double-click the little Printer icon on the right edge of the taskbar at the bottom of your screen. This icon appears whenever a document is sent to the printer; double-clicking it brings up the following dialog box:

Canon Bubble-Jet BJ-200e - Paused

| Printer | Document | View | Help |

| Documen | Pause Printing | Status | Owner | Progress | Started At |
| Microso | Cancel Printing | | | 1 page(s) | 11:59:52 AM 11/25/95 |

1 jobs in queue

habits & strategies

You never can tell when your printer cartridge is going to run out of ink. Could be in the middle of doing those tax forms that have to be mailed by midnight! Do yourself a favor and always have an extra cartridge at the ready.

To stop your print job, first highlight the name of your document, and then choose either Pause Printing or Cancel Printing from the Document menu.

WHERE TO NEXT?

Now that you're familiar with the various parts of the PC, you're ready for the next step—going inside. It's possible that you'll never have to take the cover off your computer. More than likely, however, you'll eventually want to expand or upgrade it. When that time comes, you'll be glad you've read the next chapter.

CHAPTER

3

CAUTION

Installing and Upgrading— or How to Ruin a Busy Person's Day

47

FAST FORWARD

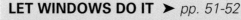

LET WINDOWS DO IT ➤ *pp. 51-52*

Use the Add Hardware Wizard in Windows 95 to set up newly installed sound cards, modems or other devices:

1. From the Start menu, select Settings.
2. Choose Control Panel.
3. Double-click the Add New Hardware icon, which starts the Add New Hardware Wizard.

DON'T MEMORIZE THE ACRONYMS ➤ *pp. 54-58*

There are expansion slots for *PCI* cards, *VLB* cards and *ISA* cards, but here's the thing: All internal cards install the same way. Just find any open expansion slot that fits, and push the card in. Carefully, of course.

RESOLVE ANY CONFLICTS ➤ *pp. 59-60*

If your newly installed hardware fails to work properly, use Windows' Device Manager to ferret out the problem:

1. Choose Settings from the Start menu.
2. Select Control Panel.
3. Double-click the System icon.
4. Click the Device Manager tab.
5. Double-click the name of your balky piece of hardware.
6. Select the Resources tab to find out if you have a hardware conflict.

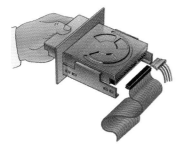

MAKE THE RIGHT CONNECTIONS ➤ *pp. 60-62*

Installing a hard drive really should be a painless experience. All you do is connect it to the system via a flat gray cable, plug it into the power supply, and hook up the little light on the front panel of the PC so you'll know when the hard drive is in use.

KEEP THINGS COMPATIBLE ➤ *pp. 62-63*

If you want to add a CD-ROM drive and a sound card, you must make sure they'll work with each other. The best way to ensure this is to buy them together in a multimedia upgrade kit.

CONSULT YOUR GUIDE ➤ *pp. 64-65*

When it comes to adding memory to your PC, it's best to let the instruction manual that came with your system be your guide. That's because different PCs take different memory chips, in different configurations. If you don't have the user's guide, call the company that made the PC.

CONSIDER A MICROPROCESSOR UPGRADE ➤ *pp. 66-67*

The cheapest way to really juice an older computer is by replacing the main CPU chip. The procedure is a lot less chancy than it used to be, and it lets you give Pentium power to a slower, 486-class machine.

If you're a busy person, you'll undoubtedly approach this chapter with a bit of trepidation. And well you should. Adding hardware to the inside of a PC can take time. You've got to take the cover off the console, get your bearings within a sea of circuit boards and cables, install the new piece of equipment, and put the PC back together again. Oh yes—you also have to make sure the new drive, sound card, or other device actually works. It's enough to make you feel like Groucho Marx, who, examining a complex legal document, said "Why, a 4-year-old child could understand this. Run out and find me a 4-year-old child! I can't make head or tail out of it."

FIRST, THE GOOD NEWS

With Windows 95, a relatively easy way to deal with PC hardware was born. It's called *plug-and-play,* and what it means is that whenever you install a new device—a printer, sound card, modem, whatever—you shouldn't have to configure it manually, or worry about it not working with the rest of your system. Windows is supposed to take care of setting up new hardware so that it doesn't conflict with any other part of your system.

Don't Start Clapping Yet

It will take time—several years perhaps—before plug-and-play becomes universal. If it's going to work perfectly, the PC itself as well as the component you want to install must be plug-and-play compatible. In the meantime, you may have to contend with devices that Windows recognizes only partially, or not at all. This is where your keen technical acumen comes in handy. In other words, you may run into trouble.

habits & strategies

The instruction manuals that come with PCs can be overly complicated, but they provide essential information for adding internal devices, memory, etc. Consult your manual before diving in.

Consulting a Wizard

Whenever you add a piece of equipment—whether it's an external device, like a printer or monitor, or something that goes inside the PC, like a modem—it has to be configured to work with Windows. Usually this means installing a software driver—either one supplied by the device manufacturer, or one that comes with Windows. If Windows recognizes your new hardware, it will tell you so the first time you start your PC after you've installed the gadget, and it will lead you through the process of software installation. If Windows doesn't recognize your new device, do the following:

Although the Wizard you encounter here doesn't have a pointed hat, it undoubtedly takes its inspiration from Merlin, whose legendary wisdom regarding swords installed in stones made him one of the very earliest hardware experts.

1. From the Start menu, choose Settings.
2. Go to the Control Panel and double-click the Add New Hardware icon. This brings up the Add New Hardware Wizard, which will offer to search your system for new hardware.
3. If that doesn't work, let the Wizard lead you through a manual installation. You'll be presented with the screen you see here, which lists various kinds of devices.

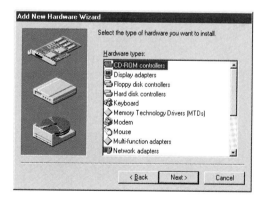

Double-click the device you want to install, and you'll see a list of specific brands and models that Windows knows how to set up. If your model isn't on the list, you can do one of two things:

• If your device came with installation software, click the Have Disk button.

- If you don't have setup software from the manufacturer, choose the Standard Installation option that Windows offers for most devices. In many cases, this will work just fine.

UNDER THE HOOD

Most people have a natural reluctance to disassemble anything electric, and with good reason. Other consumer electronics products warn you not to open them up for fear of electric shock. "No Serviceable Parts Inside" is a common label one finds on TVs, stereos, and other gizmos. But PCs aren't that way. In fact, they are intentionally designed so the user can modify them to a certain extent.

Okay, there's no sense in dragging this out any further. It's time to cut to the chase—or in this case, to the inside of the PC.

Turn Everything Off

Unplug the PC and anything connected to it, including the monitor and the printer. Don't try fooling around with the insides of your computer while it's plugged in...not only could you damage the system, you could also damage yourself. Everything unplugged? Great. Now you can remove the cover, which in most cases is held in place by three or four screws in the back. Once you've taken them out, the cover usually slides forward or backward an inch or two and lifts right off. (Consult your manual as needed for more details.)

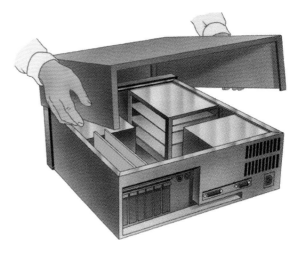

CAUTION

Once the PC is opened up, touching the insides can impart static electricity, which can badly damage the circuitry. You can build up static electricity just by walking across the floor. To avoid trouble, always touch the metal frame of the PC to discharge any static electricity before handling components.

Getting to the Bottom

Everything in the PC is connected to the motherboard, which takes up most of the bottom of a typical desktop PC case (or a good chunk of vertical space in a tower PC—usually on the left-hand side). The *motherboard* is a sheet of green fiberglass which holds the microprocessor, the RAM memory chips, the video chip (or chips), and the expansion slots for plugging in internal modems, sound cards and the like. Your hard drive, floppy drive and CD-ROM drive may also plug into the motherboard. Circuits running through the motherboard connect everything together. Here you see the inner workings of a typical PC:

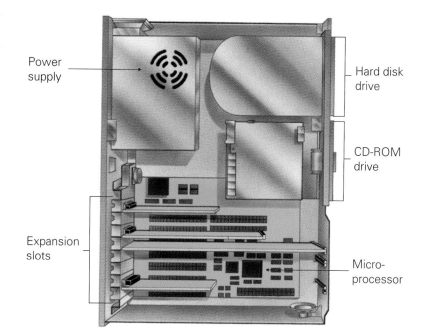

All PCs Look (More or Less) Alike

A personal computer is a complex piece of electronics, but fortunately, most of them look pretty similar inside. The expansion slots, whether vertical or horizontal, are at the left rear of the motherboard. (At least they are when the motherboard is face-up; if you have a tower machine, you can turn it...or turn your head...sideways to see what I mean.) The

♪ ♪
♪

Don't worry. ISA, VLB and PCI slots are different sizes, so you shouldn't have any difficulty matching up any card with the kind of slot it belongs in. Just make sure your PC has a PCI slot before you buy a PCI card.

power supply is at the rear on the right. The microprocessor is usually on the left side, towards the front; the internal drives are also toward the front.

ADAPTER CARDS

The most common components installed by PC users are adapter cards. These can be sound cards designed to work with CD-ROMs, video accelerators to improve monitor performance, or internal modems to connect you with online services and the Internet. Adapter cards vary in size, but have some common features:

- They are all circuit boards.
- They all install the same way—each one has edges that fit into an expansion slot inside the PC.
- Each card fits so that one side is flush with the back of the case, enabling you to plug a cable or line into it.

ISA, VLB, PCI and other Gibberish

Depending on how new your PC is, it may have several different kinds of expansion slots for adapter cards. The most common type of slot is called *ISA* (for *I*ndustry *S*tandard *A*rchitecture). In recent years, new kinds of slots have been introduced, particularly for video cards. First there was the *VLB* (*V*esa *L*ocal *B*us) slot, which offered faster throughput for video. Then came the *PCI* (*P*eripheral *C*omponent *I*nterconnect), which proved faster still. PCI is emerging as a new standard, and most new PCs have one or more PCI slots along with their traditional ISA slots. Don't you love all these names? It's like a computer version of baseball, with its ERA, MVP, RBI, etc.

Get Out Your Screwdriver

First, at the back of your PC, use a screwdriver to remove the plate from the slot you wish to use. To install an expansion card, hold it by the edges and line it up with the appropriate slot. In most cases, the fit will be extremely tight (this is necessary to guarantee a solid connection). Don't get frustrated and try to jam the card in. The best way is to work it back and forth until it's seated, and then push it completely in. Finally, screw the flange of the card to the back of the PC to hold it securely in place.

You can put an adapter card in any slot available for it. The PC doesn't care which one you use. And the card draws its power from the slot, so there's no electrical plug to worry about.

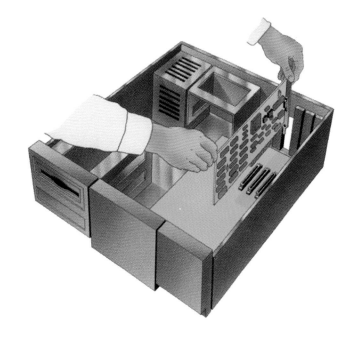

NOW THAT THE CARD'S INSTALLED...

In order for an adapter card to perform properly, it has to be configured to work with your PC. Thanks to a trend toward standardization, most cards come preset to work with most PCs, even if the system in question is not plug-and-play. But you may have to tinker a bit to get everything working right. (I always go into these things with the notion that something is going to go wrong. That way, I'm never disappointed.) Seriously, though, if you know what to look for, most problems can be corrected easily.

Setting Up a Modem

In order for a modem to work, it has to be set to a COM port. Other devices, particularly mice, also can use COM ports. Most modems come preset to work on either COM1 or COM2—the manual that came with your modem will tell you which one. To find out which COM ports are available on your PC, choose Modems from the Control Panel, then click the Diagnostics tab to display the following dialog box. The modem in this example is on COM2.

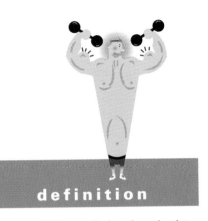

definition

COM port: *An interface that lets the PC connect with a component such as a mouse or a modem. Most PCs today come with four COM ports, but it's best, when possible, to stick to COM1 and COM2. Using the others can create conflicts.*

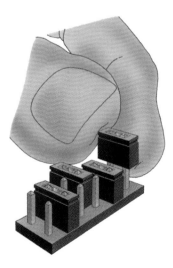

Modems Properties

General | Diagnostics

Windows detected the following ports, and has already installed the following devices:

Port	Installed
	Serial Mouse.
COM1	No Modem Installed.
COM2	Standard 14400 bps Modem
COM4	No Modem Installed.

Driver   More Info...   Help

OK   Cancel

Changing COM Ports

Switching *COM ports* usually means changing the jumper settings and/or resetting the dip switches. *Jumpers* are sets of small metal pins located on the adapter card or motherboard. Some of the pins usually have plastic covers; each of these has a metallic lining that activates the pin inside. You change the jumper settings by moving the tiny covers around to activate different pins, as shown here:

Dip switches are sets of tiny, numbered toggle switches located on the card. You reset them by moving individual switches to the ON or OFF position:

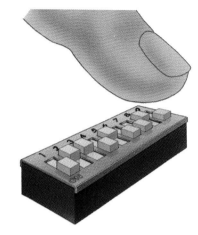

CAUTION

Your modem manual should tell you how to set jumpers or dip switches for different COM ports. If you do have to make changes, however, do yourself a favor: WRITE DOWN THE ORIGINAL SETTINGS, because once you start moving jumpers and resetting switches, you could really mess things up if you can't recall how they were in the first place.

Venturing Into Video

Another popular expansion card is the *video adapter*, often referred to as a *graphics accelerator*—another term that didn't exist a generation ago. These adapters are useful for speeding up the way your PC displays images. Here are a few things to consider before buying one:

- Don't get a card that is too good for your monitor. In other words, your monitor has to be able to handle the resolution of your video adapter. The documentation that came with your monitor should list its capabilities.
- If your PC has a VLB or PCI expansion slot, get that kind of adapter card. You can install an older ISA card, but you won't get the same performance as with one of the newer types.
- Most new PCs have video built right onto the motherboard. Older models often came with video adapter cards. If you're unsure about your computer's video configuration, check the back of the case. If the monitor plugs into one of the expansion slots, you've got an adapter card. If it plugs in at the bottom, next to the other PC connectors, you've got built-in video.

Video Drivers

In order to use a new video adapter, you'll need to install a software driver for it. Windows 95 comes with drivers for many popular video cards, and most video manufacturers include drivers of their own on floppy disks that come packaged with the cards. Here's how to manually change a video adapter:

1. From the Start menu, choose Settings.
2. Click Control Panel, then double-click Display.
3. Choose the Settings tab.
4. Select Change Display Type to bring up the following dialog box:

5. In the Adapter Type section at the top of the box, click the Change button and follow the instructions. You'll have the option of searching a list of Windows 95 drivers for one compatible with your model, or using the disk that came with your video card. You can also try one of the standard Windows drivers, which work with a majority of adapters. (Video card manufacturers often claim that their drivers work better than the ones that come with Windows, but in my experience, it's hard to tell the difference.)

**habits &
strategies**

*Multimedia games work closely
with your sound card. Many
games search your system
during installation to determine
your sound card settings.
If you've changed an IRQ or
DMA setting to avoid a hardware
conflict, make sure to configure
the game with the settings
that work.*

WHEN YOUR PC HAS A CONFLICT OF INTERESTS

Every component of the PC draws on the system's resources in order to send and receive information. If the adapter card you've just installed tries to use a resource that's already been spoken for, you have what's called a *conflict*—which likely means that your new card won't work. Three chief sources of device conflicts are actually (on a good day) avenues of system communication; they go by the mystical acronyms *IRQ, DMA,* and *I/O:*

IRQ This refers to an *Interrupt Request,* which adapter cards use to grab the attention of the microprocessor. Keyboards, printers, COM ports, and adapter cards all need IRQ lines, and if two devices try to use the same one, neither may work correctly. Your PC has only 16 IRQ lines, so it's not uncommon for more than one card to be configured with the same IRQ.

DMA Stands for *Direct Memory Access.* Devices use DMA channels to bypass the microprocessor and access system memory directly. There are only eight DMA channels in your PC, but normally only a couple of them are used by the system.

I/O Stands for *Input/Output.* Every hardware device has an *I/O address* which the system uses for sending it instructions.

Resolving Disputes

Windows 95 provides a way to discover and resolve conflicts: through the Device Manager. Suppose the new sound card you've just installed doesn't work. You may have a device conflict. (Sound cards are notorious for these, because they use IRQs, DMAs, and I/O addresses.) Here's how to identify the problem:

1. Choose System from the Control Panel.
2. Click the Device Manager tab.
3. Find the name of your sound card on the list of devices, and double-click on it.
4. Choose the Resources tab to see a list of resources currently allocated for the card, which should resemble the following list:

interface: The connection between multiple pieces of hardware, or between hardware and software, or between software and the user.

IDE: Integrated Device Electronics. *A standard interface for hard disks that enables them to operate without separate controller cards. That way, they're smaller—and cheaper— than SCSI disks.*

SCSI: Small Computer System Interface. *Very large-capacity hard disks use this interface. You can attach up to seven devices—disk drives, tape drives, etc.—to one SCSI interface. If you're short of expansion slots, this can be a real plus!*

5. If there's a conflict, the screen will identify the problem. Double-click the offending IRQ, DMA, or I/O, and you'll be able to scroll through alternatives to find one that isn't being used elsewhere.

INTERNAL DRIVES

Suppose technology whizzes right past you, and suddenly your hard disk drive is too small, or you want to add a CD-ROM (or upgrade to a faster one). Not to worry. It's a fairly simple procedure to install a device, or swap out an old one. This is particularly so because manufacturers, sensing that consumers are frightened of anything too complicated, have taken to selling kits that include all the parts, cables, etc., that you need. Some even include installation videos you can watch on your VCR.

Lots of Ways to Connect

Hard disks, CD-ROM drives, and other internal devices communicate with the PC via flat gray cables that plug into interface connectors.

Most hard disks for home PCs use the IDE interface, which lets them plug right into the motherboard. Another type of interface, SCSI, is widely used for CD-ROMs. But SCSI (pronounced *scuzzy*...ugh!) requires a special expansion card, and SCSI devices can be more difficult to set up than those using IDE.

HARD DRIVES MADE EASY

Nothing has demonstrated the rapid advance in PC technology as vividly as the evolution of the hard disk drive. Today's drives are bigger, faster, and cheaper than ever, and major manufacturers have settled on standards that let even a busy person replace an older, slower, smaller-capacity drive with a new one.

INSTALLING A HARD DISK step by step

All right, it's time to get your hands dirty. (Not! Actually, that's one of the neatest things about working with computers. It's not like working on a car; you don't have to wash up afterward.) Following is the basic procedure for replacing a hard disk:

1. Locate the old disk unit, which you can identify because it looks almost exactly like the new one. It's about 4 inches wide by 6 inches long, and less than an inch deep.

2. Loosen the screws that hold the disk in the case. Unplug the unit from the PC's power supply, and disconnect the flat gray cable connecting it to the motherboard. Also, disconnect the wire that leads to the hard disk light on the front panel.

3. Lift out the old disk unit and put in the new one. (Don't touch the circuit board on the bottom side!)

4. Attach the flat cable and the power cable to the new unit, and hook up the wire to the panel light. (New disks usually come with new gray cables, but you can use the existing one if you want.) Screw the new disk drive securely into the PC case.

CAUTION

Before you remove a hard disk
from your PC, be sure to back
up any data that you're going
to want to put on your new disk.
Simply copy the information
from your old disk onto a floppy
(or, more likely, onto a number
of floppies). Many programs—
such as Windows—will have
to be loaded onto the new disk
from scratch, so you should
make sure you have all your
program disks as well.

First and Foremost, You Format

Before you can use a hard disk, it has to be formatted, just like a floppy. Hard disks usually come with formatting software and instructions. Once the disk is formatted, you can put Windows 95 and the rest of your software on it.

Give Yourself a Boot

Always keep a floppy that you can use to start your PC in case your hard disk has problems booting up. When you first load Windows 95, it asks you if you want to create a Startup disk. Do it. But suppose your PC came with Windows preloaded, and you don't have a Startup disk? No problem. Just do the following:

1. Get yourself an empty floppy.
2. Go to the Control Panel in Windows 95, and double-click Add/Remove Programs.
3. Choose the Startup Disk tab to pull up the following dialog box, and take it from there.

ADDING A CD-ROM

Installing an internal CD-ROM drive is similar to adding a hard disk, although a CD-ROM drive fits in through the front of the case. You may need to attach rails to the sides of it so it can slide into grooves in the opening. A good CD-ROM drive will come with all the necessary cables and hardware. As with a hard disk, a CD-ROM drive connects to an interface cable and plugs into the PC's power supply.

Compatibility Is Key

In addition, you need to attach an audio wire from the drive to your sound card. It can be a matter-of-fact affair. But you could run into trouble if your CD-ROM drive isn't compatible with your sound card. The best way to ensure compatibility is to buy the same brand CD-ROM and sound card. Better yet, get them together in a multimedia upgrade kit. This guarantees you compatibility and saves money, because the components sold together cost less than you'd pay for them individually.

Choosing an Interface

The problem is that there is no standard interface for CD-ROM drives. Many brands use SCSI cards, some are IDE, some have their own special cards, and others plug directly into any compatible sound card. If you're replacing one CD-ROM drive with another, just make sure the new one uses exactly the same interface as the old one.

OTHER INTERESTING HARDWARE

Depending on what you use your PC for, there are a number of other devices, both internal and external, that you can add on. Here are just a few examples:

Internal Tape Backup Drive Yes, believe it or not, magnetic tape—like what you use in your Walkman—can hold computer data. An internal tape drive installs like a CD-ROM or floppy drive, in a bay that has an opening in the front panel of the PC. Tape drives can store hundreds of megabytes of data on tape cassettes, and are especially attractive because working with them is much faster and more convenient than backing up onto floppies. They still can be slow, however, if you're backing up a big hard disk, and restoring your data also can take time.

*A few inconsiderate PC makers
force you to remove hard drives
and cables to gain access to
SIMM slots. If you're faced with
this situation, it might be worth it
to have the memory installed.
Most computer stores will do
this for you (although they may
also charge you $50 or more for
the service).*

Removable-Cartridge Hard Drive Sometimes called a *Zip
drive* (after the popular model by Iomega that you see here), this
compact device connects either to a parallel port (the same kind of port
your printer uses) or to a SCSI interface.

Zip drives use removable disks, about the size of floppies, that hold 100
megabytes or more of information each (as compared to 1.44MB on a
floppy). The downside is that they only use cartridges made specifically
for them—they can't handle odinary floppies.

Scanner This useful gadget lets you copy pages of paper into
your PC, graphics and all. A typical scanner is about the size of a small
printer, and connects via a SCSI interface or a dedicated expansion card.
You can edit a block of scanned text— just as you would any word
processing file—using special *Optical Character Recognition* (OCR)
software. In addition to standard-sized scanners, there are also hand-held
models available that can process small graphical images.

ADDING MEMORY

As I mentioned earlier, you need at least 8MB of RAM to run
Windows 95 efficiently. If you often run more than one program

Your PC might not automatically take advantage of any new RAM chips you install. The system should display the amount of memory it thinks is available each time it starts up. If it's not finding the added RAM, go into the system setup program (usually accessible during startup) and change the settings to reflect the new total amount. Consult your PC user's guide for details.

simultaneously, or if you use huge, graphics-intensive programs, you'll want to consider expanding your RAM to 12 or 16MB.

SIMMs Aren't So Simmple...

RAM usually comes in *SIMMs,* which stands for *S*ingle *I*n-line *M*emory *M*odules. Why they can't just call them RAM chips is a mystery. It seems that everything in the computer has to have an acronym. Anyway, different brands of computers accept different kinds of SIMMs, and all the SIMMs in a PC have to have the same format. Your PC's instruction manual should tell you which kind of SIMMs you need and what configuration to use when expanding. For instance, to add 8MB, you may need to use two 4MB SIMMs rather than one 8MB SIMM. (Don't ask.)

...But Installing Them Can Be a Snap

Your manual also should give you detailed instructions for installing SIMMs. Basically, it's a simple procedure that goes like this:

1. Locate the memory slots on the motherboard. They are usually near the front, but may be obscured by other components.
2. Handle the SIMM chip by the edge. Line it up so it faces in the same direction as any SIMMs already installed. (The way the chips are made, it's pretty hard to install them backwards.)
3. Insert the chip at a 45-degree angle to the slot, as pictured here. Then just pull it forward until it snaps into place. Voilá!

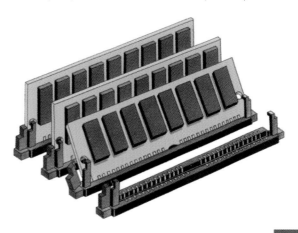

CAUTION

You can't just pop any upgrade

chip into any computer.

Like everything else having

to do with PCs, compatibility

is crucial. Make sure the

upgrade chip you get is

designed for your PC. If it isn't,

you're going to be heading back

to the store in a sour mood.

It's also not a bad idea to have

this major upgrade stuff done

by a professional, since if you

botch it, you could damage

your whole system.

UPGRADING YOUR CPU

The single best way to improve overall performance of your PC is to swap out the microprocessor for a faster one. Several companies now sell CPUs that replace older 486 chips and can more than triple the performance of an older system. Intel even has a Pentium Overdrive chip that replaces a 486 chip and adds Pentium-level speed. (Other chipmakers may soon offer Pentium-class upgrades.) You also can upgrade an older 386 PC with a chip that boosts it to 486 levels. But with the 486 now considered an entry-level machine, this honestly doesn't make much sense. In today's high-powered world, you're probably better off just donating your old 386 to charity and buying a Pentium system.

It's Not Always Easy

If you bought your PC within the last couple of years, it probably has a ZIF socket that makes it easy to upgrade the microprocessor. *ZIF* stands for *Zero Insertion Force*. You just lift a lever near the side of the socket, and the old chip lifts out. Then you can insert the new one, and lock it in by pushing down the lever.

That's easy enough. But if you don't have a ZIF socket, it can get dicey. You'll have to remove the old CPU with a special puller tool that grabs the chip on two sides. Then press the new chip in carefully, so as not to damage the pins on its underside. And you may have to change some

PCMCIA: Personal Computer Memory Card International Association. *This name tag has the honor of being perhaps the longest acronym in personal computing. PCMCIA cards come in three thicknesses, which fit into Type I, Type II, and Type III slots. Most new notebooks have a Type III slot that can accommodate one Type III card (the thickest) or any two of the other types.*

switches inside your PC. Check the manual, or call the company that made your PC for up-to-date information on microprocessor upgrades.

AUGMENTING A NOTEBOOK

When it comes to add-ons, notebook PCs are way ahead of full-size systems. Instead of having to open up the case and rummage through the innards, you simply plug in a credit-card-size device called a *PCMCIA card*, and you're in business. The cards fit into the side of the notebook, as shown here. PCMCIA cards can be modems, sound cards, RAM—almost anything. And the Windows 95 Add Hardware Wizard works with PCMCIA cards just as it does with other devices.

Convenience Carries a Price

As with almost everything about notebook computers, PCMCIA cards are more expensive than comparable devices for regular PCs. In addition, it's extremely difficult to upgrade a notebook's microprocessor.

HAD ENOUGH ABBREVIATIONS?

Okay, that'll do it for hardware. Let's turn our attention now to the other half of the PC equation: software. This is the stuff that let's you work and play and learn—and spend way too much time in front of your computer.

Part 2

SOFTWARE

Software Lesson #1: Windows, What Else?

FAST FORWARD

START A PROGRAM ➤ *pp. 76-78*

The easiest way to use Windows is to start at Start:

1. Click the Start button, which is located in the lower-left corner of the screen, on the taskbar.
2. Point at Programs.
3. Find the program you want on the Program menu, or on one of its submenus.
4. Click the name of the program to start it.

GET HELP ➤ *pp. 79-80*

Help is just a few mouse clicks away:

- Select Help from the Start menu to enter the world of Windows Help.
- If you're working in a program, choose Help from the menu bar at the top of the screen.
- If you're still in a panic, try pressing the F1 key. In many Windows programs, this will open a Help file.

SEE WHAT'S IN YOUR PC ➤ *pp. 81-82*

My Computer and Windows Explorer both let you view and manage files and folders inside your PC.

1. Access My Computer by double-clicking the My Computer icon on the desktop.
2. To open Windows Explorer, choose Programs from the Start menu and choose Windows Explorer from the list that appears, or right-click My Computer and choose Explore.

CREATE A DESKTOP SHORTCUT ➤ *p. 83*

1. In either My Computer or Windows Explorer, right-click a file or folder and drag it to the desktop.
2. From the menu that pops up, choose the Create Shortcut(s) Here option.

Now that you've created the Shortcut, you can double-click it at any time to immediately access the file or folder.

Recycle Bin

Add/Remove Programs

COPY A FILE ➤ *pp. 84-85, 86-87*

1. In either My Computer or Windows Explorer, locate the file you want to copy and right-click on it.
2. Choose Copy from the shortcut menu that appears.
3. Right-click the folder where you want to copy the item.
4. Choose Paste. That's it! The file is copied.

DELETE A FILE, FOLDER, OR PROGRAM ➤ *pp. 85, 87*

1. In My Computer or Windows Explorer, right-click the item you want to delete. A shortcut menu will appear.
2. Choose Delete. The item you've chosen will be moved to the Recycle Bin, where it will stay temporarily in case you change your mind later and decide to retieve it.
3. If you decide to eliminate the item from your system entirely, you can empty the Recycle Bin. Simply double-click the Recycle Bin and, from the File menu, choose Empty Recycle Bin.

INSTALL NEW SOFTWARE ➤ *p. 88*

1. Choose Settings from the Start menu.
2. Go to Control Panel.
3. Double-click Add/Remove Programs.
4. Click the Install button.
5. Follow the instructions to install the program.

It's quite possible that in the last year, more has been written about Windows 95 than about the search for a cure for cancer. That may be a little disconcerting, but it's not surprising. More than 80 percent of the PCs in the world now run on Microsoft's operating system software, of which Windows 95 is the latest incarnation. Windows is an extraordinarily complex and sophisticated piece of engineering, and no attempt will be made in this chapter to explain it all. The focus here, as in the rest of this book, is on cutting through a foreboding labyrinth of possibilities to arrive at easy ways to use Windows 95 for everyday tasks. Anyone who wants a more in-depth resource should check out Ron Mansfield's *Windows 95 for Busy People*, which hit the bookstores earlier this year.

THE DESKTOP

When you first turn on your PC, you're greeted by a mostly empty screen called the *desktop*, shown in Figure 4.1. There are a few icons down the left side, and a thin strip across the bottom called the *taskbar*. At the left edge of the taskbar is the Start button, which readers of previous chapters are familiar with. At the right edge of the taskbar is an area featuring a clock—just so you can always feel pressured to get your work done.

Getting Started

Clicking the Start button displays the Start menu, which gives you access to the basic features of your system and lets you start programs.

Icons —

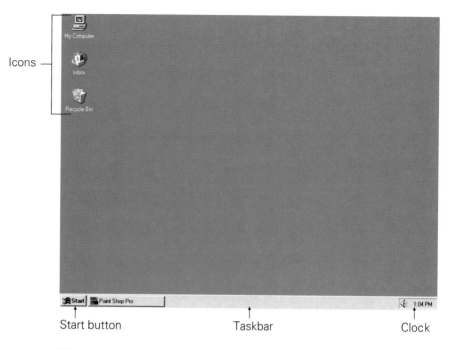

Start button   Taskbar   Clock

Figure 4.1 The Windows desktop

Depending on how your PC is set up, the items on the menu may vary, but it should look something like this:

Following is a rundown of what the different choices mean.

Programs Pointing the mouse at Programs displays a menu of the programs and program groups on your PC. Pointing to a program group brings up a menu of programs within the group. To start a program, click its name.

Documents Displays a list of recently used documents. You can open any document just by clicking its name.

Settings Presents menus labeled Control Panel, Printers, and Taskbar. These are the gateways that let you make basic modifications to Windows and to your system

Find Gives you ways to find files if you forget their names or where they are. You can search by filename, or by text contained in a file.

Help Displays Windows' main Help screen, which lets you find information in a number of ways; you can use a table of contents or an index, or you can search by specific topic.

Run Gives you a straightforward way to start a program simply by typing its name. For instance, to launch Excel (a spreadsheet program), you just type **excel** and press ENTER. The Run option also can be used to install new software.

Shut Down Lets you safely close Windows prior to turning off your PC.

The Shut Down option on the Start menu offers you the option of restarting the computer. This, in effect, lets you reboot your PC without having to physically turn it off and then back on. The Shut Down button also lets you restart in DOS mode, which is necessary in order to play some DOS-based multimedia games.

Taking Windows to Task

The primary benefit of the taskbar is that it lets you easily move between different programs and documents that you are running simultaneously. Whenever you start a program or open a file, a button for it appears on the taskbar and stays there until you close the item. You can switch between various program and document windows by clicking these buttons—which is a heck of a lot faster than closing one program and then opening another one.

Tinkering with the Taskbar

The taskbar is a nimble little fellow. For instance, you can change its position on the screen just by dragging it with the mouse. You can put it on the top or either side if you don't like it along the bottom. You also can modify the taskbar so that it's always visible, or use a feature called

Auto hide, which displays the taskbar only when you point the mouse at it. To change the options for the taskbar, use the Taskbar Properties dialog box, shown here:

You can display this dialog box by right-clicking on any empty section of the taskbar, and then clicking Properties. (You can also open the dialog box by clicking the Start button, pointing to Settings, and clicking on Taskbar.) The Taskbar Properties box also lets you add or remove items from the Start menu and other menus that cascade off of it, such as Programs and Accessories. Just click the Start Menu Programs tab, and follow the instructions.

Windows' Version of 911

Everybody needs a helping hand once in a while. Luckily, software makers are responding by providing sophisticated Help files within the programs themselves. These files are starting to take the place of cumbersome manuals (although there isn't a Help file alive that can replace this book!). Here are several ways to get help using Windows and Windows programs:

- For help with Windows 95 itself, click Help on the Start menu. This displays a dialog box that lets you browse through a table of contents or an index, or search for help on a specific topic.

definition

properties: *Settings that determine how individual Windows elements look and behave. Nearly every item in Windows has properties, which you can modify by using the item's Properties box. The easiest way to access a Properties box is to right-click the item and choose Properties from the short menu that pops up.*

- Help on Windows programs, such as word processors and spreadsheets, is available within the programs themselves. Almost every program features a Help menu on its menu bar at the top of the screen.
- If a window has a small question mark button in the upper-right corner, you can get a description of any item in the window by clicking the question mark, then clicking the item, as shown here:

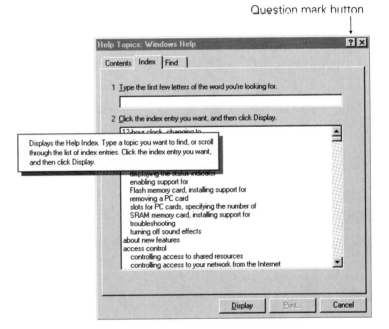

SHORTCUT

If you're really in a hurry for assistance, try pressing F1; *this will usually bring up a program's Help screen.*

Answer Wizards

Some programs designed for Windows 95 have a feature called the Answer Wizard, which can be opened through the program's Help menu. The Answer Wizard lets you ask questions in your own words. Then, picking out key words from your question, the Wizard guides you to the answer.

FOLDERS AND FILES

Windows 95 uses a workplace metaphor to give you an understanding of how software is stored inside your PC. Files, including any documents you create, are shown in the form of icons, which are contained in yellow folders. To manage things, you have two tools at your disposal: My Computer and Windows Explorer. Each in its own way lets you see how files and folders are arranged, and gives you the ability to copy, move, delete, rename, and do other stuff to your files and folders.

Inside My Computer

My Computer, a new feature in Windows 95, gives you a graphical view of what's inside your PC. Folders in My Computer are arranged in levels, which means there can be folders inside other folders. When you double-click My Computer on the desktop, you see the uppermost level, shown here, which includes your PC's storage drives.

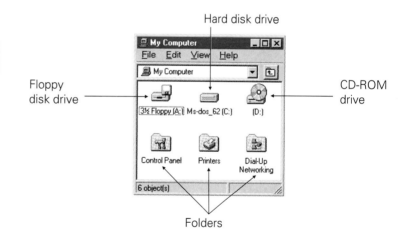

Hard disk drive

Floppy disk drive

CD-ROM drive

Folders

To find out what's on a drive or folder, double-click its name.

Icons differ in appearance according to what kinds of files they represent, or which programs are used to create them. Open any given folder and you may see an assortment of subfolders and icons. The Winword folder, for example, contains assorted files for Microsoft Word for Windows 95:

habits & strategies

You can change the way My Computer and Windows Explorer display files, altering the size of icons and including details about the files. To modify the view, use—what else?— the View menu in either My Computer or Windows Explorer. Or use the buttons at the right end of the toolbar, again in either My Computer or Explorer.

A New Age of Exploration

Windows Explorer is a spiffed up version of the File Manager inherited from earlier versions of Windows. Perhaps because My Computer is the new kid on the block, Explorer doesn't have its own icon on the desktop. You can access it from the Program menu on the taskbar, but an easier way is simply to right-click My Computer and then click Explore. Windows Explorer divides the screen into two panes. On the left are the folders (which were called "directories" in previous versions of Windows). Click on any folder, and the files contained in it appear in list form on the right, as you can see in this example:

SHORTCUT

For many operations, Windows Explorer is actually easier to use than My Computer. That's because My Computer usually requires you to open more than one window to accomplish a task, while in Explorer, it can all be done in the same window.

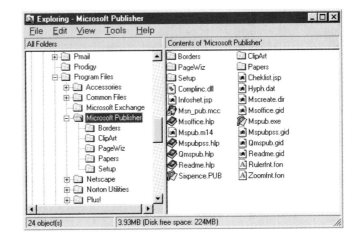

MANAGING YOUR AFFAIRS

Using Windows involves more than just gawking at all the neat pictures. To work effectively in Windows, you need to be a technological housekeeper. As you put more and more software on your PC, you're going to want to move files around inside the system, copy them, delete them and so on. Common procedures include copying a file from your hard disk to a floppy, or moving a file that has accidentally been put in the wrong folder. Stuff happens. Housekeeping is a dirty job, but somebody has to do it—in this case you! And the worst part is, you can't say "I don't do windows."

Taking a Shortcut

One of Windows 95's most convenient features is the Shortcut. A Shortcut is an icon that gives you instant access to a frequently used folder or file. This can save lots of time that you might otherwise spend rummaging around inside My Computer or Windows Explorer, or clicking your way through the Programs menu, to get to what you want. Shortcuts can go right on the desktop, where you can open them by double-clicking them. You can recognize a Shortcut icon by the little arrow in its lower-left corner.

habits & strategies

In addition to putting Shortcuts on the desktop, you also can put them in folders. For example, you can create a folder to be used by someone in your family, and put Shortcuts in it for documents he or she frequently uses.

PUTTING A SHORTCUT ON THE DESKTOP step by step

1. Use My Computer or Windows Explorer to find the folder or icon you want.
2. Right-click the file or folder, and, holding the mouse button down, drag the icon to the desktop.
3. Release the mouse button, and a menu pops up. Choose the Create Shortcut(s) Here option. Your new Shortcut will appear on the screen—and it will stay there until you decide to delete it.

81

Creating a New Folder

There will definitely be times when you want to create new folders. Say, for instance, you're working on a detailed project and you want to keep the files for it together in one folder. No problémo. In either My Computer or Windows Explorer, click on the place where you want the new folder to be. Then choose New from the File menu, pick Folder, and finally give your new folder a name.

Renaming Files and Folders

At some point you may decide to change the name of a file or folder. To do so, right-click the file or folder in question, and select Rename from the menu that appears. You can then type in your new name right over the existing name. Another way is to click the file or folder to select it, then click it again to highlight the name, and type in a new one.

Copying and Moving Files and Folders

You can use either My Computer or Windows Explorer to copy or move a file or folder. In My Computer, follow these steps:

1. Locate the item and right-click on it.
2. From the shortcut menu that appears, choose the operation you want to perform—either Copy to copy the item, or Cut to move it.
3. Find the folder where you want the item to go, and right-click on it.
4. Choose Paste from the menu that appears. The icon for the file or folder you've selected will appear in its new location, and your window should look something like this:

To copy or move something in Windows Explorer, do the following:

1. Locate the item in the right pane of the window and right-click on it.
2. From the shortcut menu that appears, choose Copy or Cut.
3. Right-click the folder in the left pane where you want to place the copy.
4. Choose paste from the menu that appears. The icon for the file or folder you've selected will appear in its new location.

Getting Rid of Stuff

To delete a file, folder, or program, you use the same techniques that work for copying and moving. Right-click the item you want to kill, and choose Delete. When you delete something from your hard drive, it goes to Windows 95's Recycle Bin, a temporary holding area that gives you a chance to change your mind and undelete things if you want to. The Recycle Bin has its own icon, which looks like a wastebasket, right on the desktop:

Changing Your Mind

To take a file or folder out of the Recycle Bin and put it back where it was before you decided to delete it, select the reprieved item (or items), then choose Restore from the File menu.

Taking Out the Trash

Discarded files and folders sitting in the Recycle Bin take up the same amount of disk space they occupied before you trashed them. To free up that disk space, you have to empty the bin. But beware! When you do so, it kills your files for good. To empty the Recycle Bin:

1. Double-click the Recycle Bin icon.
2. Choose Empty Recycle Bin from the File menu.
3. Confirm your choice in the following dialog box:

CAUTION

When you delete items from a floppy disk, they don't go into the Recycle Bin. They just go away. But at least Windows displays a confirmation box asking if you're sure you want to go through with the deletion. (A confirmation box also appears each time you empty the Recycle Bin.)

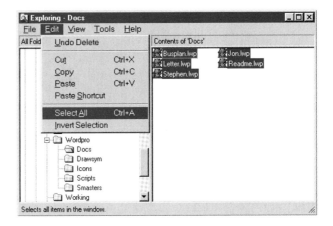

Managing Multiple Files

If you want to, you can copy, move, or delete many files at a single time. Windows Explorer is the best vehicle for this. You can select multiple folders by clicking them while you hold down the Control key (CTRL). If you want to select all the files in a folder, click the folder, then choose Select All from the Edit menu. This will highlight every file in the folder, as shown here:

You can then manipulate the files the same way you would handle a single file, by right-clicking any one of the selected files and using shortcut menu options.

Copying to a Floppy

"Don't copy that floppy." That's the software industry's slogan for discouraging software piracy. But it's perfectly all right to copy something onto a floppy. In fact, it's one of the best ways to save and protect your data. To copy *to* a floppy, follow these steps in either My Computer or Explorer:

1. Right-click the file or folder you want to copy.
2. Choose Send To from the shortcut menu.
3. Make sure there's a floppy disk in the A drive, then click 3½ Floppy (A).

It's much easier to copy,

move, and delete files using

Windows Explorer than it is with

My Computer, which requires

that you open more than one

window to get the job done.

In Windows Explorer, you can

work in one window, simply

dragging files from one side

to the other.

It's Okay to Be a Drag

An easy way to handle files is to drag them with the mouse. In My Computer or Windows Explorer, you can move files from one location to another on a hard disk simply by dragging them to new folders and dropping them in. To copy them, just hold down while you drag. You can also use this technique for the following procedures:

- Delete any file or folder by dragging it to the Recycle Bin.
- Drag a program or folder to the Start button to create a new item on the Start menu. You'll then be able to open the item with a single click.
- Print a document by dragging it to a printer Shortcut on the desktop.

The rules change when you're copying or moving things between different drives. To copy something from a hard disk to a floppy, for instance, just drag the item to the floppy icon in My Computer or Windows Explorer. To move something, hold down SHIFT while you drag. Why did Microsoft make it so complicated? Go ask Bill Gates.

The Keys to Speed

If you want to work really fast, try using keyboard shortcuts. These usually combine CTRL with another key to perform an operation. Shortcuts in many Windows programs let you copy (CTRL-C), cut (CTRL-X), and paste (CTRL-V) text and objects, as well as open (CTRL-O), save (CTRL-S), and print (CTRL-P) your documents. Available shortcuts are noted in drop-down menus, such as the Edit menu in Windows Explorer:

Keyboard shortcuts

GETTING YOUR WORK DONE IN WINDOWS 95

Windows 95 works with other software programs to help you accomplish myriad tasks, from writing letters and reports to doing your taxes and tracking your investments. There are literally thousands of Windows-compatible programs on the market, for business, education, and entertainment. Windows 95 works best with programs designed for it, but it will also work with programs developed for older versions of Windows

Installing Software

As with so many other operations, Windows 95 has automated the process of installing new software. Here's how you do it:

1. From the Start menu on the taskbar, choose Settings.
2. Go to the Control Panel.
3. Double-click Add/Remove Programs, which brings up the following dialog box:

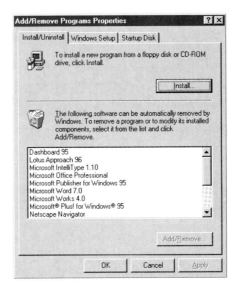

SHORTCUT

A fast way to install software is to select Run from the Start menu, and then type the command for the installation program. If your program came on floppy disks, the command usually will be either a:\install *or* a:\setup. *If it came on a CD-ROM, you can try substituting* d *for* a. *Sometimes, however, installation programs are buried in folders on the CD. Then it's easier to use the Add/Remove Programs routine.*

4. Click the Install button, and Windows takes it from there.

The Basic Look and Feel

Windows 95 imbues all programs with a similar look and feel. There's always a *title bar* at the very top of the screen, letting you know what program you're working in. Below that is a *menu bar* containing all the usual suspects, including File, Edit and Help. There are usually *scroll bars* down the right side and along the bottom of every window, so you can use your mouse to scroll through a document. And many programs feature *toolbars* that let you perform common tasks with a single click of a mouse button. In Figure 4.2, you can see the window of a typical program—in this case, Microsoft Word for Windows 95.

Take a look at the upper-right corner of the screen, and you'll notice six little square buttons. Actually, these are two identical rows, each with three buttons. The lower buttons are for shrinking or expanding the window that contains whatever document you're working on, and the upper row is for sizing the program window itself.

- Clicking the left button *minimizes* a program or document, making it disappear from the screen. However, a button for the item remains on the taskbar. Clicking this button restores the window to the screen.

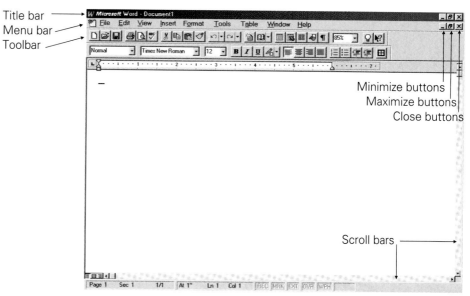

Figure 4.2 A program window containing Microsoft Word

- The middle button is for expanding or reducing the size of a window. When a program window is expanded, or *maximized*, it takes up the whole screen. This is the normal mode for programs like word processors. When a window is reduced, it takes up less space, which allows you to work with more than one window at the same time. Viewing multiple windows can be useful when you're comparing information in two documents, or when you need to move data from one window to another.

- The right button, the one with the X in it, closes the program or document altogether, with a single click. X's are always used this way. That's why dead cartoon characters have X's in their eyes.

Naming Documents

In programs designed specifically for Windows 95, you can give documents long filenames like The Great American Novel (which this book isn't). Keep in mind, though, that if you're working with a program designed for an earlier version of Windows, your filenames are limited to eight characters, such as "Great", or "American"—perhaps with three-character extensions, as in "Novel.doc". Anyway, to name a document, choose Save As from the program's File menu, and enter the name.

Using the Clipboard

Copying, cutting, and pasting aren't just for moving files and folders around. These techniques are also quite useful for rearranging text and graphics in a document. Every time you use the Cut or Copy function in one of your documents, Windows takes whatever you have selected and puts it on the *Clipboard,* which is an unseen holding area. Then you can paste it somewhere else, either in the same document or in an entirely different one—even one from a different program. All Windows programs have the Cut, Copy, and Paste options listed in their Edit menus, which makes the Clipboard a sort of universal Windows tool.

SHORTCUT

Once you've given a document a name, you can save it at any time by choosing Save from the File menu, or by clicking the Save button on a toolbar, or—in most programs—by using the CTRL-S *keyboard shortcut.*

CAUTION

Every time you move a chunk of text or graphics to the Clipboard, it replaces (and obliterates!) whatever chunk was there before. The Clipboard is just a place for temporarily storing information while you move it.

There is another Windows Accessory, called Notepad, which does much the same thing as WordPad, only not as well. Notepad provides a quick way to edit simple text files, such as some Windows system files, that require no formatting.

WINDOWS GOODIES

Windows 95 comes with a number of built-in programs, a few of which can be truly helpful. These programs are located in the Accessories menu, which you can access by selecting Programs from the Start menu. Following is a rundown of a few of the more noteworthy Windows accessories.

Go Figure

Need a calculator, but don't have one handy? No problem. Simply call up the Windows calculator, which looks and acts just like a regular calculator, except that it doesn't need batteries. Here's what it looks like:

Get a Word in

WordPad is a rudimentary word processor that's good enough to use for writing letters and other simple documents. You'll learn more about WordPad in the next chapter.

Time to Play!

Ask any bored executive what's the most impressive thing about Windows, and the answer probably will be "Solitaire!" It's a great diversion, healthier than many, and you can even change the decoration on the back of the cards. (Just choose Deck from the Game menu.) Who could ask anything more of a PC?

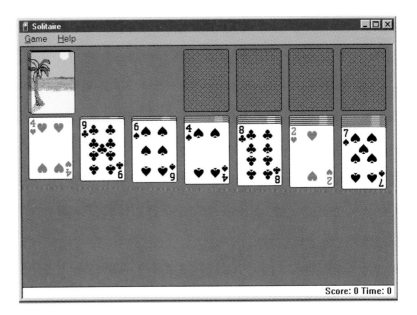

WHAT'S NEXT?

I know, Solitaire is a hard act to follow. But now that you're familiar with Windows, it's time to take the plunge and dive into a few software applications. First up: word processing.

Getting Your Word's Worth: Word Processing Made Easy

Winword.exe

FAST FORWARD

PICK THE RIGHT PROGRAM ➤ *pp. 98-100*

Heavy duty word processors such as Microsoft Word for Windows 95 offer loads of features that can satisfy any writing requirement. In fact, they may have more power than you need. A less expensive program, such as the word processor in the integrated suite Works for Windows, may fulfill your requirements nicely.

Cut	Ctrl+X
Copy	Ctrl+C
Paste	Ctrl+V

COPY OR MOVE SOMETHING ➤ *p. 104*

1. Select the text or graphics you want to move by highlighting it with your mouse.
2. From the Edit menu in any word processor, choose Cut (to move text) or Copy. Or right-click the highlighted text and pick one of those options from the shortcut menu that pops up.
3. Place your insertion point where you want the text to appear.
4. Choose Paste from the Edit menu, or from the shortcut menu after right-clicking.

B *I* <u>U</u>

FORMAT TEXT ➤ *pp. 106-107*

1. Highlight the text you want to change.
2. From the Formatting toolbar button in any word processor, click the B button to **boldface**, the *I* button to *italicize*, or the U button to <u>underline</u>. Or use any combination of them.

Times New Roman ▾

- 𝕋 Algerian
- 𝕋 Arial
- 𝕋 Arial Black
- 𝕋 Arial Narrow
- 𝕋 Arial Rounded MT Bold
- 𝕋 Arrus BT
- 𝕋 Baskerville
- 𝕋 Bauhaus 93

CHANGE FONTS ➤ *pp. 108-109*

1. Highlight the text you want to change.
2. Open the drop-down font list on the Formatting toolbar and pick a new font.
3. Open the drop-down font size list and choose a size for the type.

GO WILD WITH CLIP ART ➤ *pp. 109-110*

1. In WordPerfect, choose Image from the Graphics menu.
2. In the Insert Image dialog box, locate the filename of the clip art image you want.
3. Double-click the filename. The image appears on the screen, along with a graphics toolbar for editing it.

Importing a graphic image into a document is fundamentally the same procedure in all word processors. For example, in Word for Windows, you select Picture from the Insert menu, then use the Picture dialog box to locate your image file. You can also use the Windows Clipboard from any Windows-based word processor to copy and paste graphics.

CHECK YOUR SPELLING ➤ *pp. 112-113*

1. In Word for Windows, click Spelling on the Tools menu, press the F7 key, or click the Spell Check button in the standard toolbar.
2. If the spell checker questions a word that you know is spelled correctly, choose Ignore. If it catches you in a mistake, select the correct spelling from the list of suggestions and click Change.

Nearly all word processing programs offer spell checkers, which all work pretty much the same way. To access spell checking in Word Pro 96, for instance, select Check Spelling from the Edit menu, press CTRL-F2, or click the Spell Check button.

PREVIEW YOUR DOCUMENT ➤ *pp. 114-115*

You have two options for checking out the way your pages will look before you print them:

- Choose Print Preview from the File menu Print.
- Click the magnifying glass button on the standard toolbar.

95

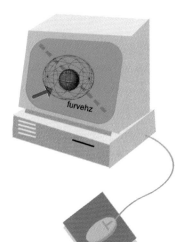

People use PCs more for word processing than they do for anything else. And that's natural enough. After all, the PC has replaced the typewriter. Also, word processing is just about the easiest thing you can do on a PC. Even a total technophobe can type a letter and print it. But heavy duty word processors definitely aren't for the computer illiterate. Over the years, competition has driven software developers to add feature upon feature to word processors, until today they are among the most sophisticated programs around. It's unlikely that you'd use more than a small portion of what one of these industrial strength programs can do. So the trick is to find a word processor that meets your needs without grossly exceeding them.

MAKING THE RIGHT CHOICE

Which word processor should you use? Depends on your requirements. If your writing is limited to letters and memos, you might manage nicely with the word processor that's built into Windows 95. On the other hand, for heavy duty work such as writing a book or a long report, you'll probably need a stand-alone word processor such as Microsoft's Word for Windows (the program used to write this book). If your needs aren't quite that great, you might consider a word processor that comes with one of the integrated software suites, such as Microsoft Works.

WordPad: The Bare Bones Model

Click the Start button, point to Programs, then point to Accessories. In the Accessories list you'll find WordPad, which is shown in Figure 5.1. WordPad is the successor to Write, the basic word processor in Windows 3.1. It lets you set margins and control the way text looks on the page. You can change type fonts, use bold facing and

*In addition to WordPad, Windows
includes a really basic text
editing program called Notepad
(which can be found in the same
list of accessories as WordPad).
Notepad doesn't have any
formatting capabilities, but it's
great for editing DOS and
Windows system files such as
Autoexec.bat, Config.sys, and
System.ini—files your PC needs
to run some DOS and pre-
Windows 95 programs.*

Figure 5.1 The WordPad utility in Windows 95

italics, and center text. You can even include graphics. Before you get
too jazzed up, however, you should know that there are a lot of things
you can't do with WordPad. You can't number pages, use headers or
footers or check your spelling. There's no thesaurus either.

Microsoft Works: The Next Level

One of the best kept secrets in the software industry is that most
people probably don't need to spend $300 or more on a Cuisinart of a
word processor. For less than $100, you can get a really good one. How?
By buying an *integrated business applications suite* such as Microsoft
Works for Windows 95. An integrated suite combines a serviceable word
processor, a database, a spreadsheet, and a communications program
into one package. The word processor in Microsoft Works gives you
just about everything a busy person could want—spell checking, a
thesaurus, etc. It even does something that more expensive programs
don't do: When you open the drop-down list of fonts in the toolbar, it
displays the actual type styles, as you can see in the following example.
(Most programs just give you a list of font names.)

If you're buying a new PC, you may not even need to buy Works. Many computer makers throw it in as part of the software they bundle with their PCs.

definition

business applications suite:

A group of major applications bundled and sold together for far less than you would have to pay to buy the programs separately. The programs in a suite share a common look and feel, and information can be shared easily among them. Microsoft Office includes Word for Windows, the Excel spreadsheet and, in the high-end version, the Access database.

The Luxury Models

The high end of the word processing market is dominated by three players—Microsoft's Word for Windows, WordPerfect (now owned by Corel), and Lotus Word Pro. Word for Windows is the most widely used, and Microsoft was the first to upgrade its flagship word processor for Windows 95. (Lotus followed with its Word Pro 96 product for Windows 95, and at this writing, a Windows 95 version of WordPerfect is planned for release in May of 1996.) All of the Big Three offer a plethora of features, including outlining, footnoting, the ability to generate an index, and other requirements for people writing long and complex documents.

How Microsoft Wiped Out the Rest

In case you're wondering how Word for Windows got to dominate the word processing field, here's what happened. WordPerfect used to be Number 1 with its DOS word processor. But, predictably, Microsoft was much quicker to develop its word processor for Windows. As a result, Word for Windows is now the market leader. Microsoft also sells Word for Windows 95 as part of Microsoft Office which, by early 1996, held nearly 90 percent of the market for business applications suites.

Striking Similarities

Regardless of which word processor you use, the basic layout of the screen—and the way you work—will be pretty much the same. There's the main white area—a virtual piece of typing paper—in which you write. Across the top is the main menu bar, and below it are one or more toolbars that let you perform common functions with the click of a button. Major word processors usually have two toolbars: a standard one for stuff like opening, saving, and printing files, and one for formatting text. To learn what a particular toolbar button does, just place the mouse pointer on it, and an explanation pops up—as in this example using Word Pro:

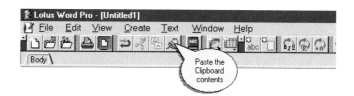

The Compatibility Game

Here's the problem: Every word processor saves documents in its own particular file format. You can't just open up a WordPerfect document in Word for Windows and start using it. First you have to convert it, using a special filter. All the major word processors include filters for other formats, but because new versions of the products are always coming out, it's no sure bet that your word processor will be able to use documents created with any given product. For instance, Word for Windows 95 can convert files from WordPerfect, but not from Word Pro. To open a document created with another file format—or save a file to another format—do the following:

1. Choose Open or Save As from the File menu.
2. Click the drop-down file type list for a list of available formats, as shown in this example from Word for Windows, and select the format you want.

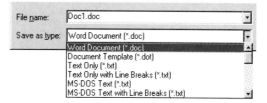

THE FUNDAMENTALS

All word processors work basically the same way, so if you learn how to use one, you'll be able to use any of them. It's sort of like driving a car, except you don't have to buy gas or pay for insurance.

Getting Around

Figure 5.2 shows a document window in Word for Windows 95. There are several ways to move around in a word processing document:

- You can use the mouse to drag the button in the vertical scroll bar up and down. You also can scroll by clicking the arrows at the ends of the scroll bar.
- The arrow keys on the keyboard move the *text insertion point* up or down by one line of text at a time, or back and forth one character at a time.
- Pressing the PAGE UP or PAGE DOWN key moves the document up or down, one screenful of text at a time.
- The HOME key takes you to the beginning of a line, and the END key to the end of a line.
- By pressing the CTRL and HOME keys together, you go right to the start of the document in most Windows programs. CTRL-END takes you to the end.

What Happened to the Mouse Pointer?

When you move the mouse into the white working area, it changes into a pointer that looks like this:

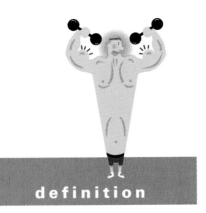

definition

text insertion point: *The point in your document where text appears when you type. On your screen, the insertion point is indicated by a blinking vertical line.*

I ◄——— Mouse pointer

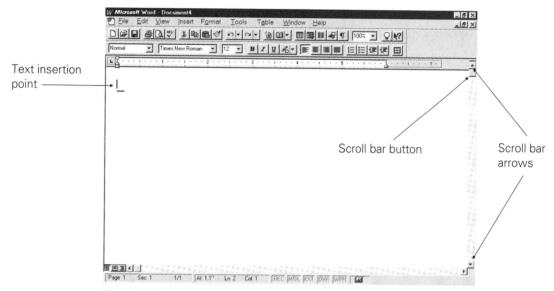

Text insertion point

Scroll bar button

Scroll bar arrows

Figure 5.2 Tools for navigating a document in Word for Windows 95

Clicking the pointer anywhere in the text area moves the insertion point to that location. The mouse pointer, meanwhile, lets you move the insertion point, select text, click buttons, and so on. When you move the mouse pointer out of the working area, it turns back into the familiar white arrow.

Making a Selection

Whenever you need to do something to a block of text—move, copy, or delete it, or change its font or italicize it, for instance—you first have to select it. The most popular way to do this is to point to the beginning of the block, then drag the mouse to the end of it. As an example, if you were to select the first sentence of this paragraph, it would look like...well, just turn the page and you'll see what it would look like!

SHORTCUT

Some word processors have an option in the Edit menu that lets you select an entire document. To select from the insertion point to the end of the document, press CTRL-SHIFT-END.

Whenever you need to do something to a block of text—move, copy, or delete it, or change its font or italicize it, for instance—you first have to select it.

Cut, Copy, and Paste

The routine for these procedures is the same as in other Windows programs. To copy or move text, select it and choose the appropriate action from the Edit menu: either Cut (to move the text), or Copy. Then click at the point where you want the text to go, and choose Paste from the Edit menu. Or, you can use several alternative methods once you've selected the text:

- Use the right mouse button to perform the actions on the highlighted text, thereby bypassing the Edit menu.
- Use drag-and-drop. To move text this way, place the mouse pointer anywhere in the highlighted text and drag it to its new location before releasing the mouse button. To copy text, do the same thing while holding down the CTRL key. (Make sure to release the mouse button before you release the CTRL key.)
- Use keyboard shortcuts, which are really fast. Press CTRL-C to copy something, CTRL-V to paste, or CTRL-X to cut text you want to paste someplace else.

Finding and Replacing

Nothing's more frustrating than knowing you've got to change a word or phrase in your document...only you can't find it. That's where the Find and Replace functions come in handy. These are usually found in the Edit menu. The following example shows you how Find and Replace work in WordPerfect. Type in what you want to find, and if you want to replace it, type that in as well.

**habits &
strategies**

The Find and Replace feature is great for changing something that you've screwed up throughout a document. Like maybe you've spelled your boss' name wrong a dozen times. You can fix all 12 instances at once by using the Replace All option.

Now is the time for all good men to come to the aid of their party.

Find and Replace Text

Type   Match   Replace   Direction   Action   Options

Find:
good

Replace With:
<Nothing>

Find Next
Replace
Replace All
Close
Help

The Undo Safeguard

Suppose you delete a paragraph and then decide you want it back again. Happens to the best of us. With most word processors, you've got a safety net. It's called Undo, and it's usually the first item in the Edit menu. Once you undo something, you can redo what you've undone by clicking the Redo function, which appears right below the Undo function. (Usually, both Undo and Redo are also available as buttons on the standard toolbar. This is starting to sound like a Woody Allen routine. The point is, word processors give you plenty of chances to change your mind.)

Changing the View

Most word processors are set to default to a view size of 100 percent. At this setting, the text in your document appears onscreen at about the same size that it would on paper. If the type is too small for you to read easily—or conversely, if you want to see more of the page on your screen—use the Zoom feature in the View menu. Word processors give you a choice of sizes: 75 percent of normal, 100 percent, 150 percent, etc. You also can set a custom size if none of the listed settings suits you.

FORMATTING

By default, word processors are set up so that if you just start typing, your document will look like a business letter. But there are lots of ways to change the way a document looks. You can modify the layout of a page, the elements of a paragraph, and the appearance of the text. By taking advantage of the powerful formatting tools in a Windows word processor, you can make your prose shine—at least graphically.

The Setup

To modify the basic look of a page in Word for Windows, choose Page Setup from the File menu. This displays the Page Setup dialog box, shown here:

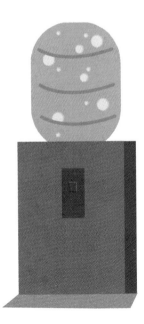

This box enables you to change the margins, paper size, and other aspects of your document.

Working with Paragraphs

A lot of formatting is done at the paragraph level—stuff like indents, line spacing, tabs, and text alignment. To fiddle with these things, you click—what else?—Paragraph in the Format menu. This will bring up the following dialog box, which lets you customize the paragraph (or selected paragraphs) that you're currently working on.

Paragraph

Indents and Spacing | Text Flow

Indentation
Left: 0"
Right: 0"

Spacing
Before: 0 pt
After: 0 pt

Special: (none)
By:

Line Spacing: Single
At:

OK
Cancel
Tabs...

Preview

Alignment: Left

Character-istics

The appearance of text is determined by character formatting. You can change the font, make letters bigger or smaller, boldface them, italicize them, underline them—you name it and the word processor probably can do it. In Word for Windows, these sorts of modifications can be done via the Font option in the Format menu. But many common formatting procedures also can be done using the Formatting toolbars that all the big word processors have. Here is the Formatting toolbar in Word for Windows:

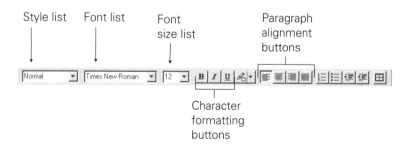

Style list   Font list   Font size list   Paragraph alignment buttons

Normal | Times New Roman | 12 | **B** *I* U

Character formatting buttons

How to Give Your Words Some Oomph

There's nothing like boldfacing, underlining, and italicizing to make text stand out. All word processors handle this the same way. Highlight the text you want to emphasize, then press the appropriate button on the toolbar—**B** for bold, / for italic and U for underline. You can even use all three at the same time, to really ***hammer home your point.***

font: The set of letters, numbers and other characters that comprise a particular typeface. The terms font *and* typeface *are often used interchangeably. Technically, that's not correct, but the fact is that nobody really cares.*

FONTS

Many Windows programs let you change type styles to achieve a special look. *Fonts* are most important in desktop publishing, but your first encounter with them will likely be in word processing. Two main varieties of fonts are used in Windows: *TrueType* and *Adobe.* Both are easy to use, although you'll need a special program called Adobe Type Manager to use Adobe-compatible fonts. Adobe fonts are used with laser printers in a process called *PostScript,* which produces professional-quality printing. But TrueType fonts give you excellent quality with less expensive printers, such as inkjets. Windows comes with some TrueType fonts.

Just Your Type

To change a font, highlight the text you want to modify, and open the drop-down font list on the toolbar. Click the font you like, and voilà! Your highlighted text takes on a whole new look. The only problem may be that you're not quite sure what a particular font looks like—so how can you decide whether to use it or not? Fortunately, every major word processor provides a way to preview fonts. If you're using Word for Windows, you can do it by choosing Font from the Format menu and clicking the font you're interested in. The preview box is at the lower right of the dialog box, as shown here:

CAUTION

Word processors, drawing programs, desktop publishers, and other programs come with myriad fonts that can stuff up your hard disk. If you find that you don't use a particular font, get rid of it. You can always reinstall it later, but there's no reason to have it hanging around just taking up space.

Regardless of the word processor you're using, you can use Windows to preview fonts. Just do the following:

1. From the taskbar, go to the Control Panel.
2. Double-click the Fonts folder.
3. Double-click the font you're interested in to get a preview like this one:

Fonts come in various sizes called *point sizes*. Standard size for a business letter is 12 points. Newspaper type is around nine points, and big headlines are 72 points or bigger. To change the size of your type, highlight it and open the drop-down size list, which is located next to the font list on the toolbar. A list of available sizes will appear; simply choose the one you want. Or you can just type in a size. In some word processors, including Word for Windows, you can even use in-between sizes like 13.5, if that size type is available and your printer will support it.

Picture This...

Word processors aren't desktop publishing programs. They lack most of the page formatting capabilities necessary for producing sophisticated newsletters, brochures, magazines, and other stuff that

clip art: *Images that come prepackaged, either in designated clip art products or as part of other types of programs. Word processors, desktop publishing programs, and drawing and painting programs usually come with an assortment of clip art.*

publishing programs do so well. But you can use graphics to liven up a word processing document such as a letter, report, or resume. Here's how you insert a *clip art* image into a WordPerfect document:

1. Choose Image from the Graphics menu.
2. Locate the image you want using the Insert Image dialog box.
3. Double-click the name of the image file. The image appears on the screen, along with a graphics toolbar for editing it. You should see something like this:

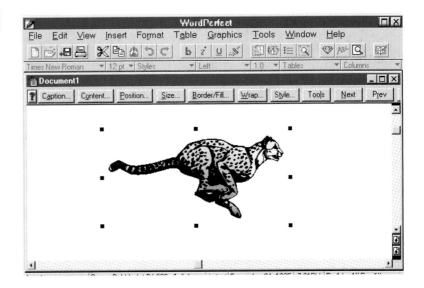

Importing graphic images is basically the same operation in all word processors. In Word for Windows 95, for example, you select Picture from the Insert menu; then you find your clip art file using the Picture dialog box. And recall from Chapter 4 that you can use the Windows Clipboard to copy and paste graphic images. The Clipboard works from any Windows-based word processing program.

A QUESTION OF STYLE

If there are recurring sections of your document that require the same special formatting, try creating an automated format, also called a *style*. There are several ways to do this, but the easiest is to format the text the way you want it, then use it as the basis for a new style.

CREATING A STYLE IN WORD FOR WINDOWS step by step

1. Format your text, including indents, fonts, and character formatting (boldfacing, italics, etc.).

2. Highlight the text.

3. Choose Style from the Format menu.

4. Click the New button to display the New Style dialog box.

5. Type a name for your style in the Name section.

6. Click OK to create the new style, which will encompass the formatting attributes in the selected text.

Once you create a style, you can apply it by highlighting the text you want to change and clicking the name of the style, which is available from the drop-down style list on the Formatting toolbar.

Templates—Formatting Made Easy

To help you along, the big word processors supply *templates*—documents preformatted to achieve a certain look. Templates can be useful, assuming that one of them meets your needs. Whenever you click New in the File menu, you have the opportunity to choose a template for the new file. Say you're using WordPerfect, and you need to write a thesis for school. You've got the choice of several templates that conform to different report styles, as you can see in this dialog box:

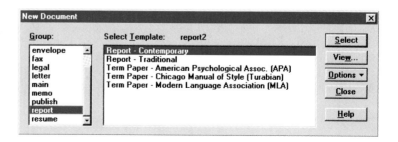

Don't put too much faith in your spell checker, because there are lots of mistakes you can make that it will fail to catch. For instance, if you leave the e *off* suite, *the result is still a correctly spelled word:* suit. *Or if you type the word* or *and inadvertently add an* e *to it, you get* ore—*also a correctly spelled word. In both these cases, the spell checker will pass right by your error.*

TOOLS OF THE TRADE

Spell checkers and thesauruses have become staples of word processing—so much so that a lot of people can't live without them. This is especially true of spell checkers, which some critics claim have led to an entire generation of kids who don't know how to spell. These kids type their school work on the computer, then let the spell checker clean it up. The flip side of this argument is, who cares if you can spell as long as you've got a spell checker available in every PC? A heated debate for sure, and one best left to another forum.

It Never Hurts to Check

Even if you're a great speller, it doesn't hurt to run your work through the word processor's spell checker—if only to catch typing errors. To check a document's spelling in Word for Windows, choose Spelling from the Tools menu, press F7, or click the Spell Check button in the standard toolbar. (It's the button labeled *ABC*.) Either way, the Spelling dialog box will appear:

Spelling: English (US)	? ✕

| Not in Dictionary: | rong |
| Change To: | wrong |

Suggestions:
wrong
Ron
Rona
Ronny

[Ignore] [Ignore All]
[Change] [Change All]
[Add] [Suggest]

Add Words To: custom.dic

[AutoCorrect] [Options...] [Undo Last] [Cancel]

If the spell checker catches a mistake, select the correct spelling from the list of suggestions and click Change. If the correct spelling isn't in the list, you can type it in yourself. If the spell checker questions a word that you know is spelled right—a proper name, for instance—just click Ignore.

When It Ain't in the Dictionary

There are certain words that aren't in word processor dictionaries—unusual proper names, for example. But you can add them to the electronic dictionary your spell checker uses. Then, whenever the spell checker finds the word spelled correctly, it won't bother you by asking about it. Suppose your mother-in-law's name is *Broomhilda*. That's not likely to be recognized by any word processor. To add it to the dictionary in Word for Windows, click Add when the spell checker inquires about it.

What's Right Is Right

Spell checkers work pretty much the same way from program to program, although the knobs and buzzers may be *slightly* different. For instance, if your word processor of choice is Word Pro 96 for Windows 95, you can run a spell check by selecting Check Spelling from the Edit menu, pressing CTRL-F2, or—you guessed it—clicking the Spell Check button. You'll find yourself clicking Replace and Skip instead of Change and Ignore, but the bottom line is, you'll be weeding out those pesky typos.

A Way with Words

Can't find the right word to express yourself? Try your word processor's thesaurus feature. Although not as comprehensive as a standard reference volume, this electronic book of synonyms can be quite helpful for the average writer. To look up a word in Word for Windows, click anywhere on it, and choose Thesaurus from the Tools menu. Or, simply press SHIFT-F7. In either case, the following dialog box will appear:

habits & strategies

The thesaurus that comes with a word processor is just a basic one. If you really want a full-fledged reference on synonyms, you need something like Microsoft's Bookshelf, a package of reference programs that includes the full text of Roget's Thesaurus.

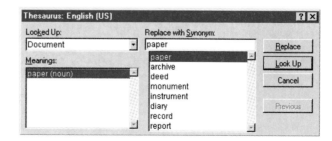

Double-clicking any word in the right-hand panel will serve up synonyms for that word. You can repeat this process, clicking on words that are close in meaning to what you want to say, until you find a synonym that suits you.

Lincoln Was Illiterate

The goofiest addition to the modern day word processor, at least in this writer's opinion, is the grammar checker. If you flat out can't write, an electronic English teacher probably can't help you. If you can write, it's just a pain in the neck. To be fair, grammar checkers can turn up bad habits in your writing, such as too much use of the passive voice. However, being institutionalized computer programs, grammar checkers give no quarter to creativity—or to really fine use of the language. The grammar checker in WordPerfect, for example, found five problems in the first two paragraphs of the Gettysburg Address, including this one:

Up for the Count

One of the advantages of the computer age is that you can precisely count the number of words you've written. That is, your word processor can do it for you. In Word for Windows, you'll find the Word Count feature listed in the Tools menu.

PREVIEWING AND PRINTING

Once you've finished your document, the next step is to print it. Modern word processors give you a *WYSIWYG* display, which stands for *What You See Is What You Get*. This means that the document should look on paper the same as it does on the screen. Ordinarily, you can see only part of a page as you work. To see the whole thing, in

habits & strategies

It's usually possible to edit while in Print Preview mode. Although the text is too small to actually work with, you have the opportunity to see exactly what a page will contain, and to reposition stuff if you want to.

Word for Windows, for instance, choose Print Preview from the File menu. Or click the Print Preview button on the standard toolbar:

Once you're in Print Preview mode, you can see how your page will look when you print it, as in the example here:

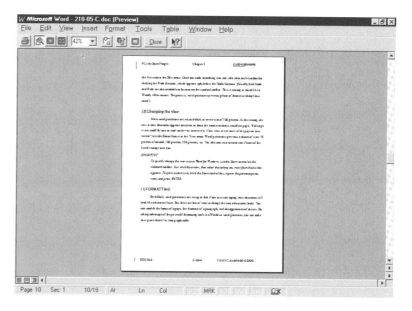

Practical Printing

As with any other Windows application, you print by choosing Print from the File menu. But you don't have to print an entire document. You can choose to print a single page, or several pages. You can even print just part of a page. Here's how you do it in Word for Windows:

1. Highlight the text and/or graphics you want to print.
2. Choose Print from the File menu.
3. Click Selection.
4. Click OK.

WHERE TO NEXT?

Now that you've got a firm grounding in basic word processing, you're ready to tackle some other popular types of business software, including databases and spreadsheets. In the next chapter, you'll even get a primer on desktop publishing. Let's go!

Software Programs That Mean Business

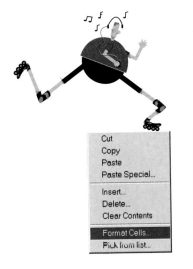

FAST FORWARD

FORMAT EXCEL SPREADSHEET CELLS ➤ pp. 122-123

1. In Excel for Windows 95, highlight the cell or range of cells you want to format.
2. Right-click on the highlighted block.
3. From the shortcut menu that appears, choose Format Cells.
4. Pick a format for the content of the cells, as well as any other formatting, such as a border around the highlighted area.

CREATE A SERIES INSTANTLY ➤ p. 123

Windows spreadsheets can automatically perform repetitive tasks, such as creating a series of numbers and filling in formulas. To create a series of months (January, February, and so on in Excel):

1. Type **January** in a cell.
2. Select that cell, and click the handle (the little black square) in its lower right corner. Notice that when you place your mouse pointer on the square, it turns into a black plus sign.
3. Drag down and/or across to cover as many cells as you think you'll need for your series.
4. Release the mouse button, and the series appears. (Now THAT'S impressive.)

TURN NUMBERS INTO A CHART ➤ pp. 125-126

1. In your Excel spreadsheet, highlight information that you want to chart, including data and text labels.
2. Click the ChartWizard button on the standard toolbar.
3. Use the mouse to select an area on the spreadsheet where your chart should go.
4. Let the Wizard help you decide what kind of chart to create, and how to dress it up to impress your boss or client.

FIND JUST WHAT YOU WANT
IN YOUR ACCESS DATABASE ➤ *pp. 129-130*

1. In Microsoft Access, click the Forms tab in the database window.
2. Click the Filter By Form button on the toolbar.
3. Enter the data you wish to search for in the appropriate field of the Filter by Form dialog box.
4. Click the Apply Filter button on the toolbar to find the records that meet your search criteria.

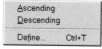

SORT YOUR DATA
IN ACCESS OR APPROACH ➤ *p. 130*

1. In Microsoft Access or Lotus Approach, display your data in table form.
2. Right-click on the column that you want to sort by.
3. In the context menu that comes up, choose whether you want to sort in ascending or descending order.

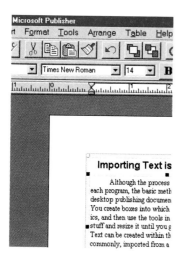

GRAB SOME TEXT
FOR A PUBLISHER DOCUMENT ➤ *pp. 134-136*

Desktop publishing software, such as Microsoft Publisher, lets you use your PC to create professional-looking newsletters, business cards, and other documents. You can easily import text from your word processing program to incorporate in a document:

1. In Microsoft Publisher, click the Text button ([A]) on the toolbar at the left-hand side of the screen. This will enable you to create a box where you want your text to appear on the document page.
2. Move the mouse pointer to the place where you want the upper-left corner of the text box to be. Click the mouse button, and then hold it down as you drag down and across the screen to the point where you want the lower-right corner to be. Release the button, and the box will appear.
3. In the dialog box that appears, locate the word processing file that contains your text.
4. Double-click the filename. Your text will appear in the text box, ready to be dressed up in Publisher.

value: A numerical entry in a cell. A value can be any kind of number, including dates and dollar figures.

formula: An instruction used to calculate a value in a cell. Formulas can be based on a relationship between two or more cells, such as the sum of the values they contain.

function: A built-in mathematical operation. All major spreadsheet programs provide functions for such things as calculating payments on a loan and finding the average value of a range of cells.

No matter what task you face, the PC can help you do it more efficiently. In this chapter we'll look at some of the major categories of business software—programs that let you calculate numbers, store and sift through mountains of information, and create truly professional-looking documents. Not everyone needs all these tools, of course. But almost any busy person can benefit from some of them.

SPREADSHEETS

Need to track sales? Come up with a business plan? Amortize a mortgage? Run a fantasy baseball league? Then you need a *spreadsheet*—the latter day equivalent of the yellow, columned legal ledgers of days gone by. Spreadsheets may, in fact, be the most versatile of all PC software programs. And the most powerful. The big league of Windows spreadsheets includes three programs: Lotus 1-2-3, which pioneered spreadsheets back in the days of DOS, Corel's Quattro Pro, and Microsoft Excel, which has come on strong in the past few years to dominate the market.

The Layout of the Land

All Windows-based spreadsheets feature the same basic screen layout, as shown in Figure 6.1. As you can see, the spreadsheet is basically a grid of rectangles, called *cells,* with letters across the top and numbers down the left side.

Following are some of the terms you'll encounter in working with a spreadsheet.

Cell This is where you enter data, which can be text, a numeric *value,* a *formula,* or a *function.* To enter information, you click a cell, which turns it into the *active cell.* A cell is named after the letter and number of the *column* and *row* that intersect there. For instance, the cell at the top left corner of a spreadsheet is named *A1.* A1 is the cell you see labeled in Figure 6.1.

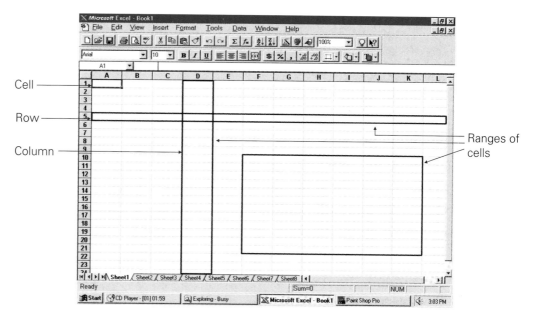

Figure 6.1 A blank spreadsheet from Microsoft Excel for Windows 95

Column A group of cells running vertically. A column is identified by the letter at the very top of the spreadsheet. In Figure 6.1, column D is highlighted.

Row A group of cells running horizontally. A row is identified by the number at the far left of the spreadsheet. In Figure 6.1, row 5 is highlighted.

Range A block of cells spread across multiple columns and/or rows. A range is identified by the letters and numbers of the cells it contains. Range F10..K21 is the one you see highlighted at the lower right of Figure 6.1.

Worksheet A synonym for *spreadsheet*. Just another name for the array of rectangles and the information it contains.

Looks Intimidating, but It's Not

Entering information in a spreadsheet is simple. You just click on the cell where you want to insert the data, then type the data in. You can even use cut, copy, and paste operations, which are very similar to those found in word processors.

121

Now, suppose you run a company that makes inflatable life rafts—let's call it SOS Inc. And you want to see how things are going with your four divisions: the United States, Canada, Europe, and Asia. Your spreadsheet will include a number of elements, including the names of the divisions, the time frames (like maybe this year's performance vs. that of a year ago), and the dollar figures for the sales themselves. (This is a pretty simple spreadsheet. If you tried to run a business this way, you'd probably need one of your life rafts.) Anyway, the SOS worksheet might look like the one shown in Figure 6.2.

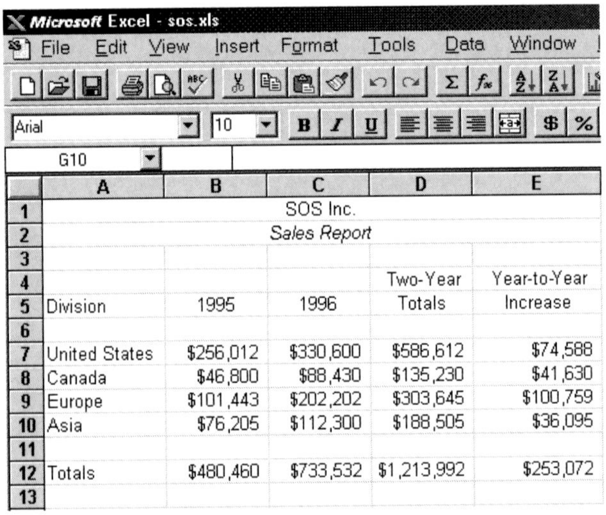

	A	B	C	D	E
1			SOS Inc.		
2			*Sales Report*		
3					
4				Two-Year	Year-to-Year
5	Division	1995	1996	Totals	Increase
6					
7	United States	$256,012	$330,600	$586,612	$74,588
8	Canada	$46,800	$88,430	$135,230	$41,630
9	Europe	$101,443	$202,202	$303,645	$100,759
10	Asia	$76,205	$112,300	$188,505	$36,095
11					
12	Totals	$480,460	$733,532	$1,213,992	$253,072
13					

Figure 6.2 A sales report for our sample corporation, SOS Inc.

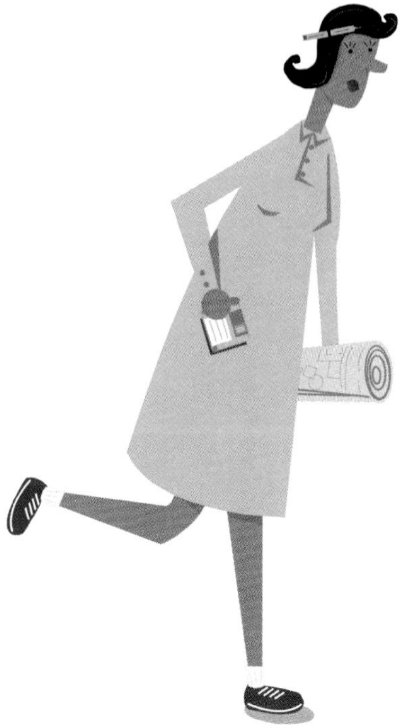

Formatting Cells

Spreadsheets usually can tell the difference between cells containing numerical values and those containing text. Still, there are times when you'll want to let the program know exactly what kind of numbers it's dealing with—currency, dates, stuff like that. It can make entering data a lot easier. For instance, if one column will have nothing but money figures in it, you can format the column so that when you type in 25, it comes out as $25.00. Pretty cool! Formatting doesn't alter the value of a cell, just its appearance. For example, you can hide decimal places without altering the number itself. To format cells in Excel, do the following:

1. Select the cell or range of cells earmarked for formatting.
2. Choose Cells from the Format menu, or right-click the highlighted cells and choose Format Cells.
3. Make your choices from the dialog box shown here:

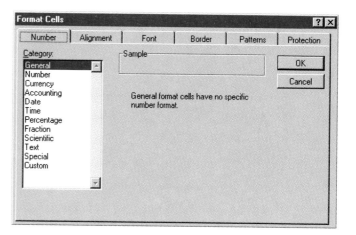

Doing the Math

Back to our SOS Inc. Sales Report! You'll notice that at the bottom of each column of numbers in Figure 6.2 is the total of those numbers. This is what makes spreadsheets so great—you can use them to do a lot of your math automatically. To add a column of numbers, such as these sales figures, you click the uppermost cell in the column and drag the mouse down, highlighting the figures you want to add up. Keep dragging the mouse until it also highlights the cell where you want to display the total. Then click the AutoSum button on the toolbar:

As if by magic, the sum of all the figures you've highlighted will appear in the bottom cell. (In our SOS report, the totals appear in row 12.)

This procedure has also been used to tally the combined 1995-1996 numbers you see in Figure 6.2. First, the figures for each year were highlighted, this time going from left to right. Then AutoSum was clicked in column D to display the two-year total for each division of SOS Inc.

Using Formulas

Column E of our fictitious spreadsheet shows the difference between sales in 1995 and 1996. For this sort of calculation, you would use a formula, typing it right into the cell where you want the answer to appear. In Figure 6.2, the figures for 1995 were subtracted from those for the following year. For example, the formula that was typed into cell E7 was **=C7-B7**. (In Excel, formulas begin with an equal sign. Don't ask why.) Then the ENTER key was pressed, which displayed the calculated value of $74,588 in cell E7.

Take Advantage of the Software

Once you've typed in a formula, you don't have to do it for every subsequent cell. Most spreadsheets let you automatically extend formulas to other cells. Suppose you were preparing the spreadsheet in our SOS example. Once Excel had calculated the year-to-year increase for the United States, you could have it quickly do the same for Canada, Europe, and Asia. Here's how:

1. Select the cell containing your formula for calculating the year-to-year change in the United States—in this case, cell E7.
2. Click the Fill handle, and drag down to include cells E8 through E12, as shown here:

E7	▼	=C7-B7		
A	**B**	**C**	**D**	**E**
1		SOS Inc.		
2		Sales Report		
3				
4			Two-Year	Year-to-Year
5 Division	1995	1996	Totals	Increase
6				
7 United States	$256,012	$330,600	$586,612	$74,588
8 Canada	$46,800	$88,430	$135,230	
9 Europe	$101,443	$202,202	$303,645	
10 Asia	$76,205	$112,300	$188,505	
11				
12 Totals	$480,460	$733,532	$1,213,992	
13				

3. From the Edit menu choose Fill.

4. From the submenu that appears, select Down. The calculated figures will appear automatically, completing column E.

In a Fill procedure, the spreadsheet program assumes that you want to adjust the cell references in the original formula so they will relate to each location you copy the formula to. So in our example, cell E8 would now contain the formula =C8-B8, cell E9 would contain =C9-B9, and so on. This little feature can save you tons of work.

Charting Your Course

One of the most amazing things about Windows spreadsheets is their ability to turn numbers into charts. Excel, for instance, can use the simple SOS spreadsheet to fashion the 3-D chart you see here, which would wow the most hard-bitten shareholder:

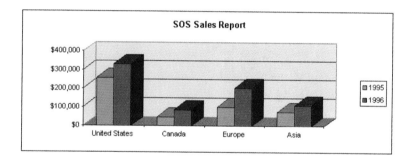

Once you create a chart with one of the newer Windows spreadsheets, it will automatically update itself any time you update the spreadsheet itself; in other words, the bars or pie segments will change in size to match your new data. How's that for a kick in the pants?

To quickly create a chart in Excel:

1. Highlight the information in the spreadsheet that you want to chart, including any text you want to include as labels. (Don't include the totals, though; they will skew the results in the chart.)
2. Start the Chart Wizard, either by choosing Chart from the Insert menu, or by clicking the Chart Wizard button on the toolbar:

Chart Wizard Button

3. Use the mouse to select an empty area on your spread-sheet (or on another spreadsheet in the workbook) where you want to place the chart.
4. Pick a chart style from the Chart Wizard's options, and let the Wizard guide you through the creation process.

Getting Rid of That Spreadsheet Look

At some point, you'll probably want to include one of your spreadsheets in a report. Wouldn't it be nice if it didn't have all those rectangles, and if you could change fonts, center some of the text, and generally make it look like you put some thought into how the thing would look? That's a big Can-Do! In this final version of the SOS report, you'll notice that the title is larger, key elements are boldfaced, there are no gridlines, and the whole thing is shaded.

SOS Inc.				
Sales Report				
Division	**1995**	**1996**	**Two-Year Totals**	**Year-to-Year Increase**
United States	$256,012	$330,600	$586,612	$74,588
Canada	$46,800	$88,430	$135,230	$41,630
Europe	$101,443	$202,202	$303,645	$100,759
Asia	$76,205	$112,300	$188,505	$36,095
Totals	**$480,460**	**$733,532**	**$1,213,992**	**$253,072**

In a nutshell, here's how to jazz up your own spreadsheets:

- Text formatting (boldfacing, type size, alignment, etc.) can be done with the buttons on Excel's Formatting toolbar.
- To turn off the gridlines, choose Options from the Tools menu, and click the View tab. Click the Gridlines box to remove the checkmark.
- To dress up a report with a border or a pattern (shading), choose Cells from the Format menu, click the Border or Patterns tab, and make your choices.

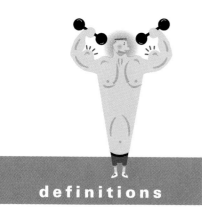

relational database: A database that stores multiple connected tables and can draw information from them simultaneously. For instance, you might search a table on inventory and another on sales to find out which products are the hottest sellers.

field: A space in a database where you put a specific kind of information, such as a name, a phone number, a date, etc.

record: A group of fields related to a single subject. In a database that tracks all your customers, for example, all the information on one customer would likely be stored in a single record.

Seen One Spreadsheet, Seen Them All

More or less, anyway. When it comes to basic operations, all the major spreadsheets are pretty much the same. Lotus 1-2-3 and Quattro Pro both can produce the kinds of examples that were created in Excel for this chapter. Once you learn the ropes in one spreadsheet, you should be able to adapt pretty quickly to any of the others.

DATABASES

If the spreadsheet is the PC equivalent of the old-style ledger, the database is the modern version of a filing cabinet. Using a good Windows database, you can create, store, sort, and retrieve reports full of information that would take hours, days, or even weeks just to locate in an old-fashioned filing cabinet.

It May Be Too Much for You

Whether you're tracking inventory, keeping lists of customers, or managing a direct mail campaign, finding a database program to handle your information is no problem. Any of the major ones—Microsoft Access, Lotus Approach, Borland's Paradox, etc.—can satisfy the requirements of a small- to medium-sized business, and will be more than powerful enough for your individual needs. If anything, you may find these big *relational databases* are too sophisticated—and too hard to learn. You might easily get by with a database that comes in an integrated suite. (Remember? We talked about those in Chapter 5. You'll learn more about them after this section on databases.)

Forms and Tables

Ah, more terms. Hey, don't worry; you're nearly halfway through the book, and you're still awake. (And at least these aren't funny-looking terms like "PCMCIA.") *Records* in a database can be entered and displayed in two ways: in a form or in a table. A *form* is a sort of template, showing you one record at a time, while a *table* gives you a list view of your database. (Tables are also called *worksheets* in some programs, such as Lotus Approach.) The following form is for a sample employee database that comes with Microsoft Access:

And here's a section of the same database in table form, which is convenient when you want to see all your records at once:

Employee ID	Last Name	First Name	Title	Title Of Courtesy	Birth Date	Hire Date	
1	Davolio	Nancy	Sales Representative	Ms.	08-Dec-48	01-May-92	507 -
2	Fuller	Andrew	Vice President, Sales	Dr.	19-Feb-52	14-Aug-92	908 V
3	Leverling	Janet	Sales Representative	Ms.	30-Aug-63	01-Apr-92	722 N
4	Peacock	Margaret	Sales Representative	Mrs.	19-Sep-37	03-May-93	4110
5	Buchanan	Steven	Sales Manager	Mr.	04-Mar-55	17-Oct-93	14 Ga
6	Suyama	Michael	Sales Representative	Mr.	02-Jul-63	17-Oct-93	Cove
7	King	Robert	Sales Representative	Mr.	29-May-60	02-Jan-94	Edge
8	Callahan	Laura	Inside Sales Coordinator	Ms.	09-Jan-58	05-Mar-94	4726
9	Dodsworth	Anne	Sales Representative	Ms.	27-Jan-66	15-Nov-94	7 Hou
(AutoNumber)							

Creating a Database

There are two ways to create a database:

- You can start from scratch. God help you if you decide to do it this way! Despite years of refinement, database creation is still just a little less painful than having your teeth pulled.

- You can let the program give you a helping hand. Microsoft Access leads you through the process with its Database Wizard, which uses templates for various kinds of databases. Other programs provide built-in templates, such as the one you see up yonder from Lotus Approach. It's designed for storing employee information:

SEARCHING WITH FILTERS IN ACCESS step by step

1. In the main window of your database program, display your database in Form view by clicking the Forms tab.

2. In Form view, choose Filter from the Records menu and click Filter By Form, or click the Filter By Form button ( ) on the toolbar. The Filter by Form window appears.

3. Enter the data you want to search for in the appropriate field. For instance, if you want to see how many beverage products your food company distributes, enter **Beverages** in the Category field, or use the drop-down list to find the category.

4. Choose Apply Filter|Sort from the Filter menu, or click the Apply Filter button ( ) on the toolbar. The program will filter the database and return the records that meet the criteria.

To Remove the filter and get your total database back on the screen, choose Remove Filter|Sort from the Records menu.

You can save Access filter

searches as queries by clicking

the Save button (🖫*) on the*

toolbar after you've selected the

criteria for your search. Queries

can be used again and again, and

can serve as the basis for reports.

Finding Information

The great strength of a database is its ability to let you search for information that meets certain criteria. It does this through *queries,* which you fill out with the information that you're looking for. Queries can be extremely complex; you can use them to search for single, exact matches, or for multiple entries that contain certain text or numbers. Microsoft Access also lets you use *filters* to search your database. This is not as sophisticated as querying, but it's easier and faster.

Sorting It Out

Another thing databases do exceedingly well is sort information. And this is a whole lot easier than querying. In either Microsoft Access or Lotus Approach, for example, do the following to sort your database alphabetically by a specific field of information.

1. In Access' Table view (or Worksheet view in Approach), right-click the top of the column you want to sort by. This highlights the entire column and brings up a context menu.
2. In Access, choose either Sort Ascending or Sort Descending from the context menu.
3. In Approach, choose Sort from the Worksheet menu. Then, in the submenu that appears, choose whether you want to sort in ascending order (A to Z) or descending order (Z to A).

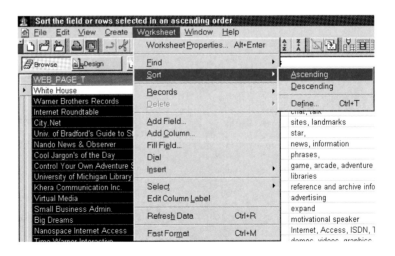

Putting It on Paper

Using queries, you can customize your database and generate all sorts of reports. You could, for instance, have the PC produce an invoice based on information in the database, or an updated report on your compact disc collection, listing recordings by artist or record label. Again, however, be aware that creating a custom report is no easy task. The database companies know that their programs can be nearly impossible to understand, so they've built in automated routines to walk you through the process of creating basic reports. Do yourself a favor and take advantage of them.

INTEGRATED SUITES

If you have a small home business, or if you just use your PC at home for family stuff, you may not need an industrial-strength spreadsheet or database program. A suite of programs, such as Microsoft Works for Windows 95, provides minor-league models of the most important business applications—along with many of the features of their bigger cousins—in a single package. In Microsoft Works, for example, you get all this:

- A word processor that has most of the main formatting features of larger programs (as described in Chapter 5), including a spell checker and a thesaurus.
- A spreadsheet that has many of the moves of Excel, including a nifty feature called Easy Calc that lets you perform common mathematical operations at the touch of a button:

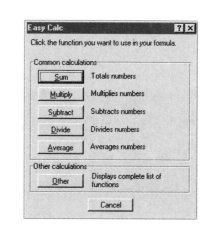

Almost every integrated suite also comes with a communications program—for connecting your PC to other computers via a phone line. Unfortunately, such programs are no help if you want to connect to a major online service or the Internet, which is what most folks want these days. For this, you need special software, which you'll read about in Chapter 12.

- A database with tables, forms, and easy-to-use queries that allows you to create reports, mailing labels, and other stuff.

So What's Missing?

If you have to do complex scientific calculations, stick with a heavy-hitting spreadsheet. And if you need a relational database—to use on a corporate network, for example—then an integrated suite is not the answer. That's because the databases provided in these suites are what's called *flat-file databases.* They're fine for manipulating data within a single file, but they can't pull information from multiple tables for reports, queries, etc., like powerful relational databases can.

GRAPHICS PROGRAMS

If your business involves technical drawings, photos, whatever, they're probably being produced, or at least manipulated, with graphics software. But before you run out and buy a fancy new program, ask yourself sincerely—are you artistically inclined? If the answer is No, a full-fledged graphics package may bring you more frustration than fulfillment. But if the answer is Yes, one of today's versatile graphics programs may open the door to wondrous possibilities. This image, for instance, was created with the ABC Graphics suite from Micrografx:

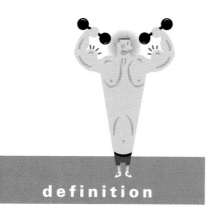

shareware: *Software distributed over online services and/or the Internet. Some shareware programs give you free trial periods, after which the software simply stops working. Others rely on your honesty. In either case, you're expected to pay for the program if you like it. But the price is always much less than for a comparable program you might buy in the store.*

Get the Picture?

The most valuable graphics software for many people is the kind that lets you use images and photos that have been created in different formats. The worst thing in the world (well, maybe that's overstating it...Woody Allen would say brain cancer is worse) is to have a great image and not be able to use it because your word processor can't import the file format. One of the best programs for dealing with graphics is Paint Shop Pro, which happens to be a *shareware* program. It allows you to import virtually any graphic image and then save it in a new format that your word processor or desktop publishing program can recognize.

DESKTOP PUBLISHING

Not too many years ago, publishing was something done exclusively by companies such as McGraw-Hill. Then along came the computer revolution, and suddenly everybody and his mother got into the act. Today, thanks to powerful software and inexpensive printers, desktop publishing has become one of the most popular uses of the PC. Most magazines, virtually all print advertising, and many newspapers are produced this way, and many individuals are using publishing software for home and business projects.

Levels of the Game

There are basically two levels of desktop publishing software. At the top are the do-everything programs, such as Pagemaker, Quark Express, and Ventura Publisher. But these programs cost in the $500 range, and give you features you might never use, such as the ability to fine-tune color for a full-color publication. The busy person who wants a professional look without the complicated extras might consider Microsoft Publisher for Windows 95. This relatively inexpensive program (under $100, street price) has given Microsoft a lock on the low end of the market, and proven to be surprisingly robust in the process.

There's Those Wizards Again!

Realizing that people know what they like when they see it, Publisher features more than a dozen PageWizards for designing everything from

CAUTION

Desktop publishing programs and big databases are among the most memory-hungry software you can get. If you intend to do graphics-intensive work with a desktop publisher, you ought to have at least 16 megabytes of RAM in your PC. Otherwise, you could spend a lot of time waiting for pages to materialize on your monitor.

newsletters to business cards. For example, there are several newsletter designs you can choose from the Newsletter PageWizard, as shown here:

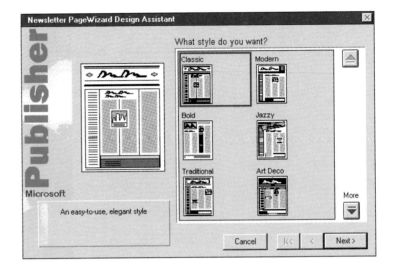

Basic Concepts

Although the process is slightly different in each desktop publishing program, the basic method of producing a document is the same. In most cases, you create boxes into which you put text and graphics, and then you use the tools in the program to move stuff and resize it until you get the look you want. Text can be created within a box itself or, more commonly, imported from a word processing program.

Formatting Text

You change the look of text in a desktop publishing program much the same way that you do in a word processor. For instance, in Microsoft Publisher, a Formatting toolbar appears across the top of the screen whenever you select a text box. Highlight the material you want to change, then use the toolbar functions to alter the font, change the type size and alignment, etc. You also can create styles for text, which are similar to the styles used in word processing programs. (See Chapter 5 to review our discussion of word processing styles.) These can come in very handy in desktop publishing, where the same styles are often used repeatedly—in a newsletter for example.

IMPORTING TEXT IN MICROSOFT PUBLISHER step by step

1. Create a box for your text. You do this by clicking the Text button (🅐) on the toolbar at the left-hand side of the screen. Then point to the spot on your document page where you want the box to begin. Press and hold down the left mouse button, and drag it down and across to where you want the box to end. Release the mouse button, and your text box appears on the page.

2. Choose Text File from the Insert menu.

3. In the dialog box that appears, locate the name of the file that contains the text you want to import.

4. Double-click the filename. Assuming you've written your text in a word processing program whose format is recognized by Publisher, the text will be converted and placed in the box.

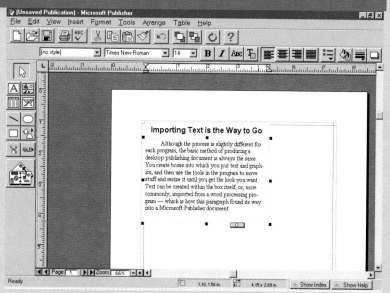

The process of importing graphics is the same, except that you create your box using the Picture button (🖼️) on the toolbar. If you want to use an image that's provided in Publisher, choose Clip Art from the Insert menu. If you want to import an image from some other program, choose Picture File.

Creating a Text Style

In Microsoft Publisher, the easiest way to create a new style is by using the Format menu and the Formatting toolbar to set up a section of text the way you want it, and then using that section as the basis for the new style. Here's how:

1. Highlight the text that you want to use as the basis for your style.

2. Choose Text Style from the Format menu.

3. Click the Create a New Style button.

4. In the Create New Style dialog box that appears, enter a name for your style. It's that simple.

To apply your new style, follow these steps:

*Documents tend to look messy
and cluttered if they include too
many different fonts. This is
especially true for newsletters.
Try to use a minimum number of
typestyles—maybe one for text
and one or two for headlines.
Sounds simplistic, but this kind
of simplicity will improve the
appearance of your document
and make it easier to read.*

1. Click anywhere in any paragraph (or highlight a block of
   text, if more than one paragraph is involved).
2. Open the drop-down list of styles on the left-hand side of
   the Formatting toolbar. You should see the name of your
   style listed there.
3. Simply select the style you've created, and you should see
   your text change accordingly.

OKAY, WHAT'S NEXT?

With major applications software out of the way, it's time to turn
your attention to other kinds of programs that are designed to help your
PC rather than helping you. These are *utility programs,* which can make
your computer run faster and more efficiently, as well as diagnose and
fix common PC problems. (Well, okay...in the long run, these programs
will help you after all.)

Utility Programs: When Your PC Needs a Tune-up...or a Doctor

FAST FORWARD

OPTIMIZE YOUR HARD DISK ➤ *pp. 142-143*

1. Click the Start button and go to System Tools in the Accessories section of the Programs menu.
2. Choose Disk Defragmenter.
3. Select the disk you want to check. You'll see a box letting you know how much your disk is fragmented, and whether you should defragment it.
4. If Windows recommends defragmentation, click Start, then get a cup of coffee.

GIVE YOUR DISK A CHECKUP ➤ *pp. 144-146*

1. Click the Start button and go to System Tools in the Accessories section of the Programs menu.
2. Choose ScanDisk.
3. Select the disk to be examined.
4. Specify whether you want a standard checkup or the thorough version, which will also check the actual physical surface of a disk. (Opting for the works doesn't cost any extra.)

KEEP YOUR SYSTEM VIRUS FREE ➤ *pp. 146-147*

If you're using windows 95, you'll need to install of a third-party virus protection program, such as Norton AntiVirus or McAfee's VirusScan95. Make sure the program you choose is up-to-date, because there are new viruses breaking out all the time! In most cases, you can get upgrades for your anti-virus software through your online service or the Internet.

VirusScan95 provides a feature called VShield that will start along with Windows and remain active in the background as you work. Once you've installed the program, you can get a progress report on VShield's activities at any time:

1. Right-click the VShield icon at the right end of the taskbar
2. From the shortcut menu that appears, choose Status to display the latest report.

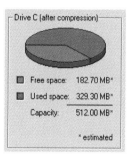

BACK UP YOUR DATA ➤ *pp. 148-150*

1. Click the Start button and go to System Tools in the Accessories section of the Programs menu.
2. Choose Backup.
3. Select the files or folders you want to back up by placing checkmarks next to them with the mouse. (You can also mark the checkbox next to a drive on the left side of the dialog box to back up the entire drive.)
4. Click Next Step.
5. Choose the destination for your backup file (a floppy drive, a tape drive, a removable hard disk, etc.).
6. Click Start Backup.

COMPRESS YOUR HARD DISK ➤ *pp. 150-151*

If your hard disk is getting full, and you don't want to take the time or spend the money to upgrade it, you can use Windows' DriveSpace utility to increase your disk's holding capacity by more than 50 percent.

1. Click the Start button and go to System Tools in the Accessories section of the Programs menu.
2. Click DriveSpace.
3. Select the drive you want to compress (most likely the C drive, otherwise known as your hard disk).
4. Choose Compress from the Drive menu, and proceed from there.

REMOVE SOFTWARE ➤ *pp. 154-156*

You can use the Add/Remove utility to uninstall some of the programs designed for Windows 95. This utility completely removes the unwanted program, along with any little traces it might otherwise leave behind to clutter up your hard drive.

1. Click the Start button and point to Settings.
2. Click Control Panel.
3. Double-click Add/Remove Programs.
4. Check the list of programs on your PC that Windows can uninstall. If the one you want is there, double-click it and follow the instructions.

The PC has spawned a cottage industry of software makers who hawk products designed to improve system performance, protect computer data, and help you fix such problems as balky hard disks. These *utility programs* were all the rage a few years ago, when DOS was still around and Windows, in its early versions, was not the most reliable system in the world. Windows 95, however, incorporates several of the most important utilities. Should you go out and buy additional utilities? The answer depends on a number of factors, not the least of which is how paranoid you are about your PC. This chapter will deal with Windows' main utilities and cover some major third-party programs that also can be useful.

CARE FOR YOUR DISK AND IT WILL CARE FOR YOU

PCs are a lot like people. When something goes wrong with one of the disks in your back, it prevents you from working normally. Same thing holds for a PC's hard disk. Disk problems are among the most common—and frustrating—things that a computer owner can face. But don't despair. Like a good medical plan, Windows offers ways to keep your disk in shape, diagnose any problems that may crop up, and easily fix some of the common ones.

Defragmenting Sounds Painful, but It's Good for Your Disk

As you use your PC, adding and deleting files and programs, files on the hard disk can become *fragmented*. Simply put, this means that data that should be stored together gets scattered around the disk. When files are fragmented, it takes the PC more time to retrieve them,

There's no rule stating how often you should monitor your disk to see if it needs optimizing. Once a month should be plenty for most folks. However, if you notice your system slowing down for no apparent reason, check the disk. If it is badly fragmented, your system's performance can be seriously impaired.

which slows down your system. You can solve this problem by *optimizing* (also called *defragmenting*) your disk.

Optimizing Your Disk with Windows

Windows 95 comes with an optimizing program called Disk Defragmenter, which lets you check your hard drive to see if it's badly fragmented, and then optimize it if necessary. Here's how to use Disk Defragmenter:

1. Click the Start button, point to Programs, then to Accessories, and then to System Tools.
2. Click Disk Defragmenter, as shown here:

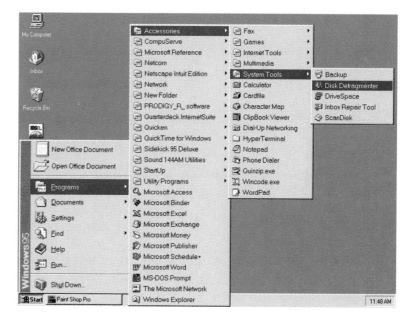

3. Select the disk you want to optimize, and click OK. (Your hard disk is the default. You also can optimize a floppy disk, but as far as I know, no one ever has.)
4. A box will appear, letting you know what percentage of your disk is fragmented, and whether you should optimize it. If you decide to go ahead and do it, click Start and the program will do the rest. Depending on how much stuff is on your disk, it could take several minutes or even longer. By clicking on Show Details, you can see a graphic illustration of the procedure, as in the following example:

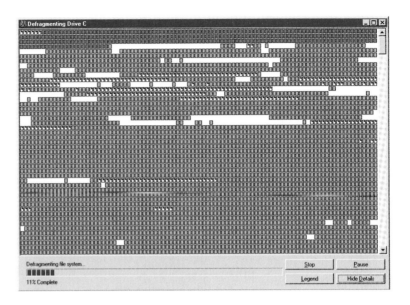

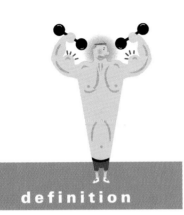

lost clusters: When a file is saved to disk, it's divided into storage units called clusters. Some files can take up dozens of clusters. If a PC is turned off before a file is properly closed, some of the clusters may lose their links to the Filename so that the system has no record of them. The result? Lost clusters.

Checking for Problems

Occasionally, you may run into disk problems that require diagnosis and treatment. Or maybe you're just the careful type who always wants to make sure everything's in tip-top shape. Windows provides a utility called ScanDisk that you can use to give your disk a checkup—and fix minor problems, such as *lost clusters*. ScanDisk can look for data errors in files and folders, and even check the actual physical surface of the disk for problems. To use it:

1. Click the Start Button and point to Programs, then to Accessories, and then to System Tools.
2. Select ScanDisk. This brings up the following dialog box:

3. Select the disk you want to scan.
4. Specify whether ScanDisk should simply look for errors in files and folders, or if you want a surface scan as well. (A *surface scan* checks for physical defects on the actual surface of the disk; it will take an extra few minutes.)
5. If you want ScanDisk to fix any errors it finds automatically, make sure the Automatically Fix Errors box is checked.

When ScanDisk finishes doing its stuff, it will report on its findings, displaying a list of statistics that nobody could possibly be interested in. The main thing to hope for is that the following message appears:

```
ScanDisk did not find any errors on this drive.
```

Automatic Maintenance

If you can't be bothered with giving your disk a regular checkup, let the PC do it for you. The Microsoft Plus! add-on for Windows 95 includes a utility called System Agent that can run ScanDisk and Disk Defragmenter when you're not using the computer. And Norton Utilities includes the Norton System Doctor, which can monitor your disk while you work and optimize it automatically if the need arises.

Rescue Procedures

Suppose your hard disk is so badly damaged that you can't access it. This will mean, among other things, that you can't start Windows. Don't panic. You may be able to solve the problem using the Startup disk you created at the time you installed Windows 95. (If you didn't create this disk, then it's okay to panic.) Assuming that you have a Windows Startup disk, put it in your floppy drive and turn on the computer. It should boot up in DOS and present you with an A:\> prompt (*A* represents your floppy drive). The Startup disk contains some useful utility files; you can see what's on the disk by typing the DOS command **dir** at the A:\> prompt. Something like the following list should appear on your screen:

```
A:\>dir

 Volume in drive A has no label
 Volume Serial Number is 1F5C-73E1
 Directory of A:\

DRVSPACE BIN        71,287  07-11-95   9:50a DRVSPACE.BIN
COMMAND  COM        92,870  07-11-95   9:50a COMMAND.COM
FORMAT   COM        40,135  07-11-95   9:50a FORMAT.COM
SYS      COM        13,239  07-11-95   9:50a SYS.COM
FDISK    EXE        59,128  07-11-95   9:50a FDISK.EXE
ATTRIB   EXE        15,252  07-11-95   9:50a ATTRIB.EXE
EDIT     COM        69,886  07-11-95   9:50a EDIT.COM
REGEDIT  EXE       120,320  07-11-95   9:50a REGEDIT.EXE
SCANDISK EXE       134,738  10-28-95   2:21p SCANDISK.EXE
SCANDISK INI         7,270  07-11-95   9:50a SCANDISK.INI
DEBUG    EXE        20,522  07-11-95   9:50a DEBUG.EXE
CHKDSK   EXE        27,248  07-11-95   9:50a CHKDSK.EXE
UNINSTAL EXE        76,496  07-11-95   9:50a UNINSTAL.EXE
        13 file(s)        748,391 bytes
         0 dir(s)         481,792 bytes free

A:\>
```

You'll notice two ScanDisk files among those listed here. To diagnose your crashed hard disk—and possibly fix your problem—type **scandisk c:** at the prompt. (The c stands for your hard disk.)

This Doctor Makes House Calls

While the Windows Startup disk can help, your hard disk may be sick enough to require a specialist. Norton Utilities has a number of good rescue and recovery programs available, including something called Norton Disk Doctor. Norton lets you create Rescue disks (floppies) that include the good doctor as well as other diagnosis and recovery utilities. Rescue disks let you:

- Repair damaged files
- Recover heavily damaged disks
- Restore the data your PC needs to start itself up

Viruses—The PC Version of "Outbreak"

PCs do indeed have a lot in common with people. They can get ruptured disks, they can slow down due to physical problems, and they can get sick. In fact, PCs can be infected with viruses. No, computer viruses aren't protein-coated pieces of DNA, but they work in ways similar to the viruses that attack our bodies. A *computer virus* is a program that attaches itself to other programs, conducting unwanted operations. Some viruses are concocted as pranks, others as a high-tech form of sabotage. There are literally thousands of these evil programs, and they can get into your computer via infected floppies or even via electronic mail and the Internet. In practice, however, viruses

definition

disk crash: *This term usually refers to some software problem that renders a disk unusable. (The good news is that these days, hard disks rarely fail mechanically.)*

habits & strategies

If you use an anti-virus program, make sure it's up-to-date. New viruses are showing up all the time, like new strains of flu. Makers of anti-virus software offer product upgrades via online services and the Internet.

rarely infect home PCs. The real danger is when they get into large computer networks, which store vast amounts of information.

Treating a Virus

Windows 95 does not have the ability to seek out and destroy viruses. This seems a little odd, especially since the previous version, Windows 3.1, included virus protection. Anyway, if you're using Windows 95, you'll have to turn to third-party virus killers, such as Norton AntiVirus, or McAfee's VirusScan. These programs can check your system for thousands of known viruses and eradicate them.

A Security Guard That's Always on the Job

McAfee's VirusScan95 for Windows 95 includes a feature called VShield that starts along with Windows and runs in the background, checking the health of files as they're used. The VShield Configuration Manager lets you decide what kinds of files to scan, when to scan, and what to do if infected files are discovered. You can choose alternatives for handling sick files by tabbing over to the Actions page:

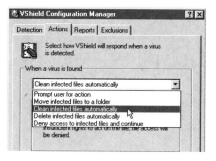

Any time you want a progress report on VShield's activities, just right-click the VShield icon at the right end of the taskbar, and choose Status from the shortcut menu. That brings up the following window. (Looks like all systems are go in this case.)

Windows Backup combines multiple files into a single file. By default, the data is compressed so that the backup file will take up much less disk space than the original files. But be aware that if you're backing up several programs, or an entire disk, your backup file can span multiple floppies.

SAFEGUARDING YOUR DATA

The mere possibility of serious disk problems should be enough to convince you to back up your important data files regularly. It's impossible to emphasize this enough. Corporations back up entire databases on a daily basis, and it just makes sense for you to do the same for the letters, reports, and other documents that you spend so much time producing on your PC. Backing up information is a pretty open-and-shut business. It consists of copying one or more files from your hard disk to a storage device that you can put someplace safe, away from your computer. For small backup jobs, use floppy disks; they're the least expensive way to go. To back up large files, or lots of data, you have a number of options.

Tape Recall from Chapter 3 that you can store your data on magnetic tape, if you have a tape drive. These are usually internal devices, like floppy drives, that start at less than $200. Each tape cassette can hold hundreds of megabytes of information.

Removable Hard Drives Also called Zip drives, after the brand name of the market leader, Iomega, these small devices are becoming quite popular. As you saw in Chapter 3 (whattaya know—that was one fine chapter!), they use special disks that aren't much bigger than floppies, but can store much, much more data. A removable hard drive plugs into a port in back of the PC. Look to pay about $200 for an entry-level Zip drive. The 100MB storage disks are less than $20 apiece.

Backing Up Your Data with Windows

Windows 95 comes with a backup utility called, logically enough, Backup. You'll find it along with Disk Defragmenter and ScanDisk in the System Tools program menu. Or maybe you won't! For some reason, certain parts of Windows are not automatically installed along with the Windows system files; Backup is often one of these missing pieces. If you don't see Backup in the System Tools menu, here's how you can install it:

1. Point to Settings on the Start menu, and then choose Control Panel.
2. Double-click Add/Remove Programs.

3. Click the Windows Setup tab.
4. Double-click Disk Tools, and click the Backup box to select it.
5. Click OK twice, and follow the instructions. (You'll need your original Windows 95 floppies or CD-ROM to complete the installation.)

Once you've got Backup loaded, the actual procedure is pretty straight-forward:

1. Click the Start button, point to Programs, then to Accessories, then System Tools.
2. Choose Backup. If a Welcome to Microsoft Backup dialog box appears, click OK to close it. (If you don't want this dialog box displayed in the future, make sure there's a check in the Don't Show This Again checkbox before you click OK.)
3. In the Microsoft Backup dialog box, select the files and/or folders you want to back up by placing checkmarks next to their names, as shown here. (Notice that the checkbox for My Documents is gray. That's because not all the files in the folder have been selected.)

Untitled - Microsoft Backup					
File Settings Tools Help					

Backup | Restore | Compare

What to back up: < Previous Step   Next Step >

Select files to back up

Name	Size	Type	Modified
Shortcut to North..	422	Shortcut	2/24/96
olompali.PUB	418816	Microsoft Pu...	1/17/96
olompali.mdb	256000	Microsoft Ac...	3/6/96
Busy11.doc	48128	Microsoft W...	2/20/96
Beck donation ac...	11264	Microsoft W...	2/4/96
agenda.doc	53760	Microsoft W...	2/18/96
COVER LETTER ...	23040	Microsoft W...	1/2/96
membercard.PUB	154112	Microsoft Pu...	2/7/96
renewal form.PUB	86528	Microsoft Pu...	1/15/96
roster.doc	56832	Microsoft W...	2/4/96
scifi.doc	11264	Microsoft W...	2/15/96

Folder tree: Eudoralite, Exchange, Microsoft Internet, MSOffice, My Documents, Netscape, pcn, Program Files, Psp, Quickenw, Sound144, Windows, Working, (D:)

File set: Untitled   Files selected: 856   10,772 Kilobytes selected

4. Click Next Step.

5. Select the destination for your backup file from the available options, which should include any storage devices attached to your PC.

6. Click Start Backup. That's it.

Restoring Backed-Up Data

Restoring your data just involves reversing the backup process. In the main Backup window, choose the Restore tab. Select the backup file to restore, choose Next Step, and follow the instructions. The backed up data will be restored. However, this process will not shrink, delete, or otherwise affect the backup file, which will remain on the removable disk or tape until you get rid of it.

DriveSpace—Windows' Magic Act

Another useful utility that Windows 95 brings to the party is DriveSpace, which lets you increase the capacity of your hard disk by 50 percent or more. It does this by compressing files when they're stored on the disk, and decompressing them when the PC needs to use them. All this happens on the fly, and although it can slow

---

COMPRESSING YOUR HARD DISK WITH DRIVESPACE step by step

1. Click the Start button, and point to Programs, then to Accessories, then to System Tools.

2. Choose DriveSpace.

3. Select the drive you want to compress.

4. Choose Compress from the Drive menu. This will bring up a dialog box showing the current status of your hard disk, and how it will change if you invoke DriveSpace. In the example you see here, the capacity of the disk would increase from about 800MB to over 1GB.

5. Click Start to compress your drive.

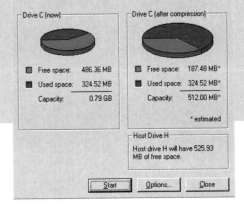

performance a bit, DriveSpace can be a lifesaver if your hard disk is getting full.

What if you compress your hard drive and then change your mind later? Don't worry. You can also use DriveSpace to uncompress your hard disk. Just make sure, before you do this, that you have enough free space on the disk for all the uncompressed data.

Zipping and Unzipping

It's also possible to compress and decompress individual files, or shrink many files together into one compressed file. This process, which is generally referred to as *zipping,* lets you store a bunch of related files—say a series of clip art images—in a single file. It can also save you a lot of disk space. For instance, a good zip program can reduce the size of a scanned graphic file by almost 100 percent—pretty impressive, considering that the file may take up hundreds of thousands of bytes to start with.

Where to Get a Zipper

File compression is offered as a feature of some utility packages, such as Norton Navigator, a Windows management product. But you also can get first-rate zipping programs by downloading them from software libraries of online services, or from the Internet. (You'll learn how downloading works in the last two chapters of this book.) One widely praised zipping program for Windows 95 that's widely available online is WinZip. This shareware program features an easy-to-use window that lets you unzip a zipped file (or zip files together). It also lets you view details of individual files inside a zipped file, as in this example:

Name	Date	Time	Size	Ratio	Packed	Path
Financ-1.hot	09/06/95	11:33	232	36%	148	
Favorite.hot	03/28/95	11:32	100	11%	89	
Entert-1.hot	09/06/95	11:39	613	59%	250	
Educat-1.hot	09/06/95	11:34	297	38%	184	
Compin-1.hot	09/06/95	11:33	186	41%	109	
Commun-1.hot	09/06/95	11:33	169	29%	120	
Cim.gif	10/19/95	15:53	1,131	22%	879	
Awcomdlg.dll	10/23/95	14:23	188,016	86%	26,736	
Airmos.exe	10/30/95	11:39	778,240	54%	357,384	
Wwwinf-1.hot	09/06/95	11:35	314	42%	181	

WinZip (Unregistered) - Mosaic.zip
File Actions Options Help
New Open Add Extract View CheckOut

Selected 0 files, 0 bytes   Total 27 files, 1,292KB

AN INSIDE LOOK

One thing Windows doesn't do well is let you see how your PC is performing. If you want details about your hardware, you have to look things up one-by-one in the Device Manager. If you're really interested in the workings of your system, you should get a third-party utility.

Norton Utilities is great for giving you easy access to information about your system through its System Information utility:

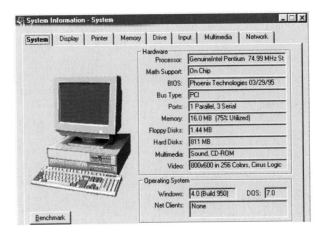

By clicking on the Benchmark button, you can even see how your system stacks up against industry standards. In the following example, it appears that my Pentium 75 is humming right along:

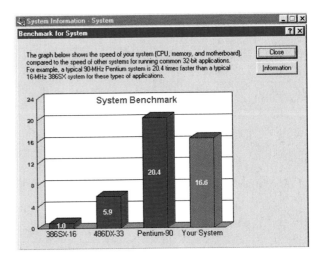

Most of the detailed information about the workings of your PC has no practical application whatever. But as you can see from the illustrations here, it looks highly impressive. If somebody asks you what the numbers mean, mumble something and change the subject.

Monitoring Performance

For accurate monitoring of many aspects of your system, a good program is WINProbe from Quarterdeck. It gives you an accounting of how the PC is using its resources, how much memory is available, and a host of other facts, as you can see here:

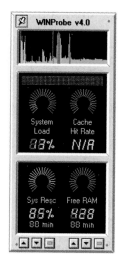

And the information is constantly being updated, so you can watch how your system manages its resources from second to second.

MEMORY MULTIPLIERS

If you frequent software stores or read PC trade magazines, you'll probably encounter programs that claim to greatly increase the amount of RAM in your system. Don't believe it. The only way to double your RAM is to do just that, by adding memory chips to your PC. Memory *doublers* mimic increased memory through compression techniques and other high-tech sleight of hand. These utilities have become popular because they're a whole lot less expensive than adding 8 megs of RAM.

Better than Nothing

Some memory enhancement programs actually can improve system performance a bit, especially if you're running multiple pro-grams at the same time with limited RAM. One memory enhancer that doesn't claim to be more than it is, and actually does a fair job, is

virtual memory: Not-quite-real memory. Windows sets aside a portion of your hard disk to act as virtual memory—a place where data can be put while a program is running so the data doesn't eat up too much regular memory. The information is then transferred back and forth from memory to the disk as needed; this process is known as swapping *the information.*

Quarterdeck's MagnaRam. It compresses data held in RAM, freeing up a little more memory and reducing Windows' use of *virtual memory*—thus giving the system a mild shot in the arm. Like other memory enhancers, MagnaRam provides statistics about how it's doing, if you care to know. The readout looks like this:

MagnaRAM Memory Details	
Memory Monitor	
Linear Memory	
Linear Memory Used: 2102336K	
Linear Memory Free: 2091968K	
Physical RAM	
Physical RAM Used: 14728K	
Physical RAM Free: 212K	
Total Physical RAM Compressed: 2450K	
Virtual Memory	
Virtual Memory Used: 1340K	
Virtual Memory Free: 10980K	
Total Virtual Memory Compressed: 2212K	
MagnaRAM Memory	
Total Memory Compressed: 4662K	
Average Compression Ratio: 1.65:1	
Virtual Memory Hard Drive Thrashing Monitor	
Swap File Hits: 167	
Swap File Hits Avoided: 1072	
Swap File Time Saved (hh:mm:ss): 00:00:05	
Close	

UNINSTALLING SOFTWARE

While Windows 95 has made it much easier to install new software, it's also made it tougher to get rid of programs you don't want anymore. You can always use Windows Explorer to remove a program's main files; simply drag the program folder to the Recycle Bin. But many programs sneak files onto other locations in your system, or place information in the Windows 95 Registry—which is a database containing information that Windows needs in order to run other software properly.

Windows 95 vs. the Competition

Some programs designed for Windows 95 can be completely removed using the system's Add/Remove Programs feature. To see whether a program can be dumped this way, try the following procedure:

1. Click the Start button, point to Settings, and click Control Panel.

2. Double-click Add/Remove Programs, and hope that your unwanted program appears on the list of programs that Windows can uninstall:

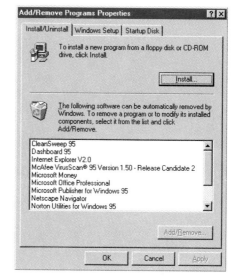

3. If the program you've grown sick and tired of is on the list, double-click it, and then follow the instructions that appear on your screen.

If a program isn't among those that Windows can automatically remove, you can get rid of it the old fashioned way:

1. In either My Computer or Windows Explorer, right-click the program's main folder. Choose Delete from the shortcut menu (or drag the folder to the Recycle Bin using the mouse).

2. But be forewarned—this method will not remove files that the program may have placed in some other folder; nor will it erase changes made to the Registry.

Time to Call In a Professional

A surefire way of getting rid of unwanted programs—and all the unwanted junk they've stuffed into your PC—is to use a program such as Uninstaller from MicroHelp or CleanSweep from Quarterdeck. Either

CAUTION

Use extreme care when removing individual files, especially when you don't know what they do. And if they're not taking up very much space, who really cares if they're in there, anyway? As the saying goes, if it ain't broke, don't fix it.

of these powerful uninstalling utilities can take a complete inventory of your Windows programs so that it knows where *all* the files and related information for a program are located. Then it can get rid of every piece of your unwanted program. The Windows 95 version of Uninstaller guides you through the process, which goes like this:

1. Click the Delete Applications button on the toolbar. This brings up a window in which you can search for programs.
2. Locate the icon for the program you want to get rid of, and double-click it. Uninstaller will then analyze the application to locate all the files and system settings related to it.
3. Once the analysis is complete, the following window will appear on your screen, displaying recommended options for removing the program. Press DELETE to complete the process.

Uninstall programs can also help clean up your hard disk by finding duplicate files, files not associated with any programs, or files that haven't been used for ages. Basically, though, they're for getting rid of unwanted programs.

DESKTOP MANAGEMENT

For some PC users, Windows' basically featureless desktop doesn't cut it. If you crave lots of information on your screen, you might consider a utility such as Dashboard from Starfish Software. This Windows add-on gives you a control panel that makes a 747 cabin look like the dashboard of an economy car. As you can see here, Dashboard gives you access to your programs, detailed system information, and even a clock and a calendar:

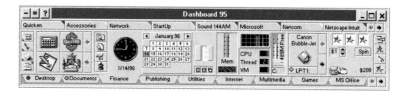

The other major desktop utility is Norton Navigator. This program adds file management tools to Windows 95's menus, such as the ability to easily compress and decompress files. It also lets you easily set up multiple desktops, so that each person in your family, for instance, can customize the Windows screen the way he or she wants it—with shortcuts to favorite programs, and so on.

WHAT'S NEXT?

In the next chapter, we're going to get personal. One of the most popular ways to use PCs is for keeping track of personal finances. You can do your checking, conduct banking online, figure your taxes, and keep track of your business contacts and appointments, all without leaving your chair. (So why not get up and move around a bit before you turn the page?)

habits & strategies

File management utilities can add useful functions to Windows, but they can also slow down your system and complicate what, for many people, is already a confusing environment. In other words, they can amount to overkill. Explore all the possibilities of Windows itself before you opt for any additional bells and whistles.

Software That Gets Close and Personal

INCLUDES

- Personal Information Managers

- Personal finance

- Preparing your taxes

- Designing a dynamite resumé

- Drawing up your will

- Charting your family tree

- Finding your way around

FAST FORWARD

CREATE AN ADDRESS BOOK ➤ *pp. 162-167*
With *Personal Information Managers*, also known as *PIMs*, you can put information about your key contacts, friends, and relatives in database-like files. You can store names, addresses, phone numbers—even birthdays—and locate them easily. And if you don't feel like buying a PIM, the Cardfile accessory in Windows 95 gives you some of those basic capabilities.

DIGITIZE YOUR CHECKBOOK ➤ *pp. 168-170*
A personal finance package like Quicken or Microsoft Money focuses the power of your PC on one of the hardest tasks known to humankind: staying on top of your checking account. With one of these products, you can balance the account in a fraction of the time it takes if you sit down with a checkbook, a bank statement, and a calculator.

BANK ONLINE ➤ *pp. 170-171*
Many major banks now let you access account information and download it directly into a personal finance program. You can also use your PC to pay monthly bills online. If your bank has joined the online revolution, you can probably sign up for online banking over the phone.

PREPARE YOUR TAXES ➤ *pp. 171-174*
Let one of the top-selling tax preparation packages, such as TurboTax or TaxCut, guide you through the miserable ritual of doing your income taxes. You can import pertinent financial data from a personal finance program, and even get valuable advice from the tax program as it figures out how much you owe—or how much Uncle Sam owes you.

GET A JOB ➤ *pp. 174-175*

With a bit of thought and layout savvy, you can create an impressive resumé using your word processor or maybe a desktop publishing program. If you'd like more comprehensive assistance with your job search, there are a number of programs available to guide you through the process. A product such as ResumeMaker, from Individual Software, can help you design an eye-catching resumé, organize your job contacts, generate cover letters, and even hone your interview skills with video simulations—all for under $50.

MAKE A WILL ➤ *p. 175*

If you're like most Americans, you don't have a written will. But take heart—you can use a home legal program to create one. Once you print it out on your PC's printer and have it signed by a notary public, it will be perfectly legal and valid in most states.

CREATE A FAMILY TREE ➤ *pp. 176-177*

Use one of the popular family tree software programs to keep track of all your ancestors. One such program boasts that you can list two million family members. (That would probably take you back to the stone age, when people didn't have PCs!) Some programs even let you include photos and biographical notes about all those aunts and uncles who send you fruitcakes for Christmas.

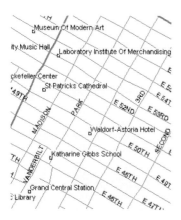

DON'T GET LOST ➤ *pp. 177-178*

These days, you can tap into the storage capacity of a CD-ROM to help you locate just about any place you need to find. With a powerful program like DeLorme's Street Atlas USA, you can search for any address in United States. Once you've zoomed in on your target, you can display the surrounding area at varying levels of distance and detail. When you've chosen the view that's most useful to you, simply print out your own custom-designed map, and off you go!

O kay, time to get personal. Which is the right and proper thing to do, considering you've bought this contraption called a *personal* computer. The PC has become an enabling tool for all sorts of personal and family-related activities. You can use it to keep track of your business and social contacts, handle your finances, and prepare your taxes. You can work up a handsome resumé if you're job hunting, or get your affairs in order by writing a legal will. There is even powerful CD-ROM-based software available that can help you pinpoint a street address almost anywhere, from sea to shining sea. What a great world this is, eh?

PERSONAL INFORMATION MANAGERS

Think about if for a second: The Rolodex on your desk or the appointment book in your bag are really just databases. Primitive and paper-based, but databases, nonetheless. With the development of the PC came a way to store the same kinds of information in a far more useful form. With a Windows PIM (*Personal Information Manager*), you can keep a list of contacts, enter your appointments, and generally stay on top of your life.

Windows' Cardfile: The Dumbed-Down Option

Windows itself includes a basic program for storing names, addresses, and phone numbers. It's called Cardfile. By today's PIM standards, Cardfile is pretty crude, but if all you want is a basic address book, it does the job. Here's how to get a list going:

1. Click the Start button, point to Programs, and then point to Accessories.
2. Choose Cardfile; this will start the program.
3. From the Card menu, choose Add.
4. Type in the name of the person you want to list, and then hit ENTER. The name you've typed will appear at the top of the onscreen card.
5. In the text area of the card, which appears below the name, fill in any information you want—an address, a phone number, a fax number, whatever. (If you plan to use Cardfile's Autodial feature—which will be explained in a minute—make the phone number the first number in the card.) When you're done, the card might look something like this:

Cardfile - NERD.CRD

File   Edit   View   Card   Search   Help

Card View   ◄ ►   **2 Cards**

```
Ned Nerd
President, Digital Digits
Phone: 707-882-9000
Fax: 707-882-9002
101 Memory Lane
Pixel CA 94949
```

Dialing Automatically

One of the nice features of Cardfile is Autodial, which automatically dials voice phone numbers—assuming that your PC has a modem and is connected to a phone line. If the information you've recorded about a person includes a phone number, simply invoke Autodial from the Card menu to place the call. One caveat, however: Autodial looks for the first number in a record. So if you follow the usual routine and enter the address before the phone number, Autodial will try to dial the address, which won't get you very far. The solution? List the phone number as the first number in every record.

CAUTION

If you're planning to create a major list of contacts, think twice before using Cardfile. You can't save them in any format other than Cardfile's own. This means that you could have trouble transferring Cardfile records to another program, such as a database.

With a Big-Time PIM, Who Needs a Secretary?

These days, Personal Information Managers represent a major category of Windows software, and with good reason. They unleash much of the power of your PC, letting you store, sort, and integrate information in ways that can make life a lot easier. Following are some examples, using two high-powered PIMs: Schedule+ (which is included in the Microsoft Office suite of programs), and Sidekick (available from Starfish Software).

More Bells and Whistles Than New Year's Eve

Both of these PIMs have calendars that offer daily, weekly, and monthly views, alarms to remind you of appointments, and To Do lists. But wait...there's more. Want to know what time it is anywhere in the world? In Sidekick, click the Earth Time clock to the right of the main working area. The following window will appear:

Although it seems like a novelty, the Earth Time feature actually is pretty cool—particularly if you have to do business with somebody in, say, Japan. You don't want to wake up an important customer at 3 in the morning, now, do you?

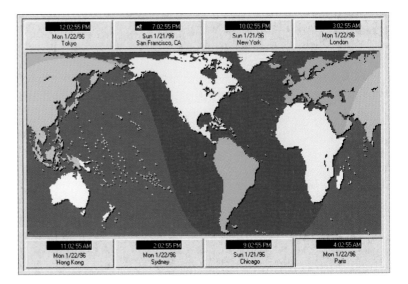

Keeping Track of Appointments

One of the features of all major PIMs is an appointment calendar that's just as easy to use as a daily planner book—and what's more, you don't

habits &
strategies

As with word processing documents, databases, and spreadsheets, you should make a point of backing up your PIM files—especially lists of addresses and phone numbers—on a regular basis. It only takes a minute to store a file on a floppy. It could take days to rebuild a list of business contacts.

have to buy new pages every year! To record an appointment in Schedule+, click the Insert New Appointment button on the toolbar and enter the information in the Appointment box. When you're finished, click OK to log the appointment on the calendar, as shown here:

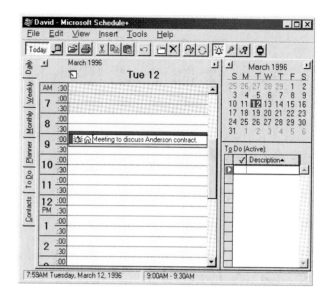

You can reschedule an appointment by dragging it to a new time slot on the day planner, or to a new date on the calendar in the upper-right corner of the window. You can even configure Schedule+ so that when it's time to get ready for the meeting, no matter what program you're running on your PC, a gentle reminder like this one will pop up:

Staying in Touch

The top-selling PIMs let you create elaborate address books (cardfiles) containing all sorts of information about people, including their birthdays. (Don't you just hate it when you get a birthday card from your life insurance agent? It's like they're saying "Happy birthday, you're still alive and we don't have to pay out on your policy!") Anyway, creating and maintaining a contact file is a pretty straightforward affair.

CREATING A SIDEKICK CARDFILE step by step

1. Click the Cardfile icon to the right of the main window.

2. Choose the New Cardfile option from the File menu.

3. Select a template from the list that appears. Templates have preset fields for names, job titles, addresses, etc. (You can add or delete fields from the templates to customize a cardfile. You can also choose None from the template list and create a file from scratch, but if you're a busy person, who needs that?)

4. Assuming you've decided to use one of the templates, enter information in the fields on the right. You can leave fields blank if you like.

5. To add another record, choose Add Cards from the Cards menu and repeat the process.

6. When you're finished adding cards, choose Save As from the File menu and give the cardfile a name.

If ever you want to remove some of the fields in your cardfile, or add new ones, choose Define Cardfile Fields from the Cards menu and proceed from there.

The Import-Export Game

Suppose you've already built a list of contacts in another program—say a database package—and you'd like to use it in your PIM. Or, on the flip side, you've created a PIM address book that you want to use in your database program. The problem is that PIMs use their own file formats,

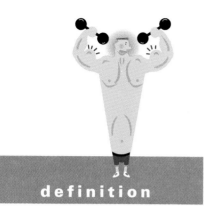

ASCII: American Standard Code

for Information Interchange.

Data files saved in ASCII can be

used by most major software

applications, including word

processors, spreadsheets, and

databases.

which usually aren't compatible with other programs. To get around this, you can save your file in a format that's recognized by the program into which you'll be importing it. Many database and PIM programs can save and read files in DBF, a common database format. And you can almost always export and import database-type files using a text-only format, sometimes referred to as *ASCII.*

Electronic Gizmos
That Work with Your PC

When it comes to staying on top of the daily routine, busy people have a lot of options these days. Companies like Rolodex sell electronic pocket organizers that use an infrared signal to transmit information directly into your PC—letting you keep the information in your computer up-to-date with the vital information in your briefcase. And there's even a watch that can receive data directly from your PC!

Dick Tracy Would Have
Been Proud to Wear It

The Timex Data Link watch looks like a regular sport-type wristwatch, but that's where the similarity ends. When you hold it in front of your PC, it can read bar codes on the monitor to download data! Using special software developed by Microsoft, you can use the watch to store phone numbers, appointments, even anniversaries (this feature could be a life saver). The main screen, shown here, lets you enter information in the Data Link software and then send it to the watch.

You can even use your Data Link watch to read information that's stored in Microsoft Schedule+.

PERSONAL FINANCE SOFTWARE

Say the word *money,* and you're sure to get somebody's attention. Which helps explain why personal finance programs are among the most popular software for PCs. With one of these programs, you can balance your checkbook, manage your stock portfolio, calculate your mortgage, and plan for future investments—like a college fund.

A Few Good Choices

There aren't too many good personal finance programs on the market—mostly because Quicken, from Intuit, has been so successful that it discourages competition. After Windows itself, Quicken is one of the top-selling software programs of all time. Other finance programs include Microsoft Money, Mecca's Managing Your Money, and Kiplinger's Simply Money. But Quicken has the lion's share of the market.

Who Needs a Manual?

One of the reasons Quicken is so popular is that it provides learning tools that make an instruction manual practically unnecessary. In the Deluxe version of the latest release, Quicken 5, there's even an audio-video tour of the program. In the following example, a wise, tiny woman shows and tells you how to work with your checking account:

In 1994, Microsoft tried to buy Intuit to get its hands on Quicken, but the government cried "Antitrust!" and Microsoft abandoned the deal. Quicken far outsells Microsoft's own Money program—one of the few areas in which Microsoft is a follower rather than a leader.

Tracking Your Finances

When you record a check or a deposit in an electronic check register, you can indicate where the money came from (paycheck, stock dividend, etc.), or what the check is for (food, entertainment, clothing, the car, etc.). In addition to helping you keep track of your income and expenses, a computerized checkbook can save you a lot of time getting a handle on your finances when tax time rolls around. In Microsoft Money, you enter the category of every payment in a window below the register, as shown here:

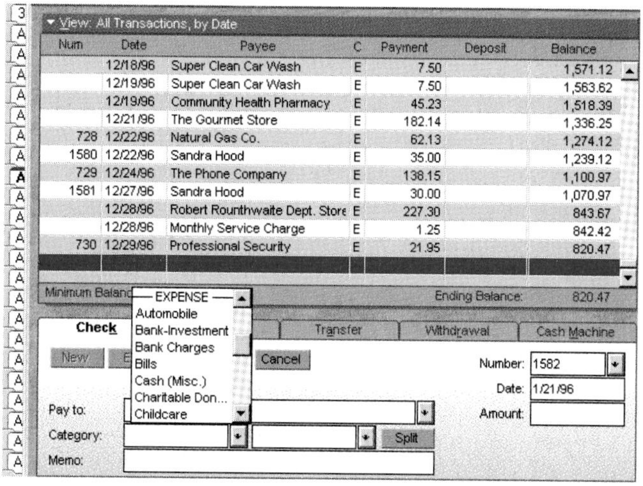

Graphic Detail

Programs like Quicken and Microsoft Money can create reports and graphics that show you your financial life in great detail. This can be exhilarating, or quite distressing, depending on your situation. You can compare different aspects, such as liabilities and assets, or income and expenses. Let's suppose you want to show your family's income and expenses, month by month, over the course of six months. Here's how you'd do it in Quicken:

1. In the HomeBase window (a new addition in Quicken 5), click Graphs.

2. When the Create Graph dialog box appears, type in a range of dates, and click the type of graph you want to create—in this case, Income and Expense.

3. Use the filter buttons at the bottom of the dialog box to filter out any information you don't want the program to consider. (If you have multiple bank accounts, for instance, these buttons let you separate them for charting purposes).

4. Choose Create. You'll see something like the following example:

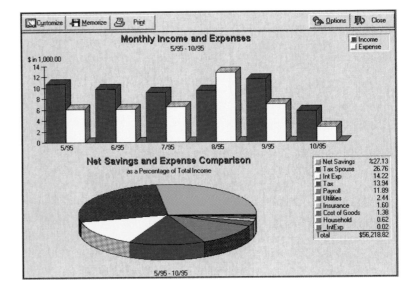

New-Age Banking

Intuit and Microsoft are helping to take PCs into a new age of online banking. Working with the major banks, they've set up ways in which you can view your accounts, download your bank statements, and even transfer money from one account to another over the phone line, using your PC. Although online banking is still in its infancy, experts in the software and banking fields believe it will become widespread in the next few years as more people have PCs in their homes.

SHORTCUT

In addition to keeping up-to-date on your account activity, you can also pay utility bills, credit cards, and big retailers online through most banks. Taking advantage of this service could cost less than the money you'd spend on stamps for mailing your checks; it also takes less time than paying your bills the old-fashioned way.

Setting Up an Online Account

To set yourself up for online banking, you need three things:

- A bank that offers the service
- A modem
- A program that works with your bank's online service. Although some banks provide their own software, more and more are letting you tap into their systems through Quicken or Microsoft Money.

First thing to do is call your bank and ask if they're into cyberspace yet, and if so, which software you should use. Usually, you can sign up for online banking over the phone, assuming that you already have an account with the bank. Next, you have to set up your personal finance software for online banking. Fortunately, both Quicken and Microsoft Money have automated this process, so it goes quickly.

Once you're all hooked up, it's a one-button operation to log onto your bank's computer and obtain account information. In Quicken, you click Online Banking in the HomeBase window to display the following window. (The bank logo you see here will change, of course, depending on which bank you're using.)

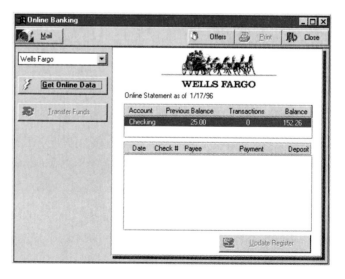

Click Get Online Data, and the program does the rest—calling the bank, requesting the information and displaying it. You then can enter the information into your Quicken checking account register, and any new entries will be marked as having cleared.

TAX TIME

Using PCs to do income taxes is becoming increasingly popular, and no wonder. Who in their right mind would sit down with a calculator and a pile of tax forms, when a software program can figure things out for you and print out the result, neat and clean, creating forms you can send directly to the IRS—as in this example from TurboTax for Windows:

TurboTax Deluxe for Windows - [Schedule A: Itemized Deductions]

File   Edit   Forms   EasyStep   Tools   Window   Help

Schedule A (Form 1040)	Schedule A — Itemized Deductions	1995

Name(s) shown on Form 1040 — Your Social Security No.

To go to supporting forms or worksheets for any line, QuickZoom from the entry field for that line

Medical and Dental Expenses

Caution: *Do not include expenses reimbursed or paid by others.*
1   Medical and dental expenses 1
2   Enter amount from Form 1040,
     line 32 .... | 2 |
3   Multiply line 2 by 7.5% (.075) 3
4   Subtract line 3 from line 1. If line 3 is more than line 1, enter -0- .... ► 4

Taxes You Paid

5   State and local income taxes 5
6   Real estate taxes 6
7   Personal property taxes 7
8   Other taxes — List type and amount
     ► _ 8
9   Add lines 5 through 8 .... ► 9

Interest You Paid Note: *Personal interest is not deductible.*

Schedule A — QuickZoom

User-Friendly and Then Some

The top-selling tax programs can be purchased in CD-ROM versions that feature the same sort of multimedia tutorials you get in Quicken Deluxe. In the case of the market leading program TurboTax, this isn't surprising; after all, it's manufactured by Intuit, the maker of

Quicken. Kiplinger's TaxCut boasts similar wizardry. These programs also come in floppy disk versions that don't have the moving pictures, but are less expensive.

Where Function Follows Form

There are two ways to use tax software: You can let the program guide you through the process, or you can fill out the various forms in any order you like. TaxCut, for instance, takes you from start to finish with a question-and-answer format that covers the entire range of tax topics, starting with the ones you see here:

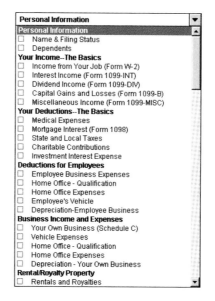

Like Having Your Own Accountant In addition to figuring your taxes, tax preparation programs can review your work. They'll let you know if you've forgotten to enter any essential information, and they can also offer suggestions on how you might save money. These programs are scrupulously honest—and they're great at math, too, so you don't have to worry about getting a letter from the IRS saying "YOU ADDED WRONG!".

But What if...? One of the biggest advantages of doing your taxes on the PC is that you can play around with various scenarios to see how they compare. For example, suppose you got married halfway

You also can buy companion programs to do state taxes. Whether or not this will be worthwhile depends on how complicated your particular state forms are. In many cases, once you do the federal taxes, the state stuff is easy, and you won't really need software for it.

through the year. Should you file jointly or separately? Using TaxCut's "What If" worksheet, you can see how the options stack up, and then make the best decision.

Electronic Filing—for a Faster Refund

If you just can't wait to get your hands on the money Uncle Sam owes you, you can file your taxes electronically. Both TurboTax and TaxCut offer this service; you can either file via modem or mail in a floppy disk. It costs under $15, and you'll have your refund in three to four weeks.

OTHER PERSONAL SOFTWARE

The PC has made it easy and affordable to do things that, in the past, were beyond the abilities of most individuals. Let's look at a couple good examples of how a computer, a printer, and inexpensive software can empower you.

Looking Good (at Least on Paper)

If you're looking for a new job, you're going to need a resumé. And in today's hotly competitive world, you'd better have a good-looking one. For well under $50 you can buy yourself a program that not only fashions a professional-looking resumé, but also can help you write cover letters and keep track of contacts, and may even use videos to take you through a simulated job interview. One such product is ResumeMaker from Individual Software:

habits & strategies

If you have a good word processor or a publishing program, you can probably create a stunning resumé without having to buy a dedicated program. Just use attractive fonts and a simple layout, and write it in such a way as to emphasize your strengths.

ResumeMaker employs (pun intended!) many of the same techniques found in multimedia personal finance programs. When you start the program, it takes you into a virtual Career Center. By clicking on different areas of the room, you can compose a letter to a prospective employer, update your contact list, and—most importantly— create your resumé. There's also a comfy-looking sofa, and when you click it...nothing happens! Maybe it's there so you can take a nap while waiting for someone to call.

Where There's a Will, etc.

Just as programs like TurboTax free you from having to go to an accountant or tax assistant, home legal programs can sometimes take the place of a lawyer. And who wouldn't rather deal with a PC than a lawyer? A program such as Kiplinger's Home Legal Advisor, for example, can help you plan your estate, prepare a will, or perhaps get power of attorney over your mother-in-law. To create a will, you first choose the type you want, and then fill in the blanks—as in the example here, for a will that distributes property to a spouse and children:

CAUTION

PC-generated wills and legal documents are recognized as valid by most states, but it pays to check, just so you're sure. And bear in mind that most legal documents have to be signed by a notary public, whether or not there's been a lawyer involved in creating them.

All in the Family

One of the most popular hobbies that the PC revolution has sparked is genealogy—keeping track of your family tree. Actually, if your family is like mine, the best thing to do would be chop down the tree and use it for firewood. But that's only my opinion. My wife, on the other hand, loves the idea of being able to trace the history of our families, mostly so our kids can know where they came from. There are several good family tree programs for Windows, including Family Ties from Individual Software. This program provides forms, like the one shown here, that make it easy to fill in information about your family. You can even include photos.

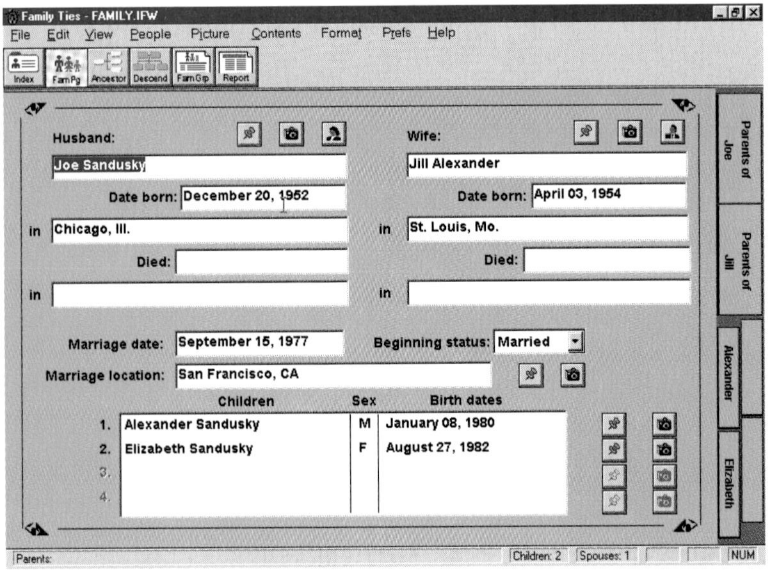

By using the tabs at the right of the window, you can choose to enter data about your children, then about your parents. Then, by clicking on the Ancestor icon on the toolbar, you'll be able to see your family tree in all its splendor, as in the following example:

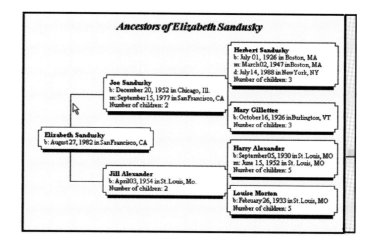

Never Ask for Directions Again

Don't you just hate street maps? The one you want is never in the glove compartment—and the worst part is trying to refold the map when you're done with it. Fortunately, the PC age has given us programs such as Street Atlas USA from DeLorme. You can use this CD-ROM to find almost any place in the United States, as long as you know the street address and zip code. Suppose you're going to New York, for example, and you have tickets for a show. Using the program's Find feature, you can pinpoint Radio City Music Hall in a matter of seconds:

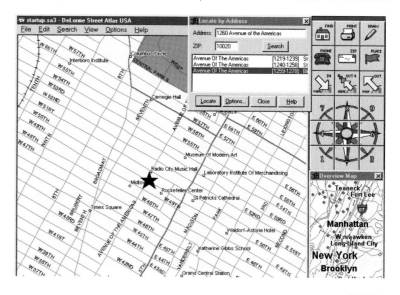

Street Atlas USA gives you several zoom levels, so you can have either a detailed view showing just a few blocks, or a view of the whole island of Manhattan. When you get the map the way you want it, you can print it out and take it with you. And because it's on a regular piece of typing paper, it's really easy to fold.

WHERE TO NEXT?

In this chapter, we've seen that many programs for home PCs are starting to take advantage of the multimedia features available on CD-ROMs. In the next chapter, you'll see how multimedia is changing education, entertainment, and the way we obtain information.

CHAPTER

9

Multimedia:
The Real Reason
You Bought Your PC

FAST FORWARD

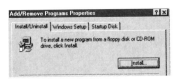

GET THE RIGHT STUFF ➤ *pp. 184-186*

To use a wide range of multimedia software, your PC should have at least a fast 486 chip and some special hardware, including:

- A CD-ROM drive (at least double-speed)
- An internal sound card—preferably a 16-bit model for good stereo sound
- Stereo speakers designed for use with a PC

INSTALL A MULTIMEDIA PROGRAM ➤ *pp. 186-187*

Place the multimedia CD in the CD-ROM drive. If the CD features AutoPlay, it will initiate the installation process all by itself. If it doesn't, take the following steps:

1. Click the Start button on the Windows taskbar.
2. Point to Settings, then click Control Panel.
3. Double-click Add/Remove Programs.
4. Click Install, and follow the instructions that appear.

RUN MULTIMEDIA FROM DOS ➤ *p.187*

A few multimedia games and other programs still run from DOS. To run a DOS session within Windows:

1. Click the Start button and point to Programs.
2. Click the MS-DOS Prompt icon. A window will appear in which you can run a DOS session. You can have either a small window or a full DOS screen; press ALT-ENTER to toggle between them.

To leave Windows and switch to DOS mode:

1. Click the Start button and choose Shutdown.
2. Click "Restart the computer in MS-DOS mode?".

When you're ready to end your DOS session, you can get back into Windows by typing **exit** at the DOS prompt.

PLAY A MUSIC CD ➤ *pp. 188-189*

Put an audio compact disc into the CD-ROM drive. With most new drives, Windows should recognize a music CD and use AutoPlay to start the CD Player. To start the CD Player manually:

1. Click the Start button.
2. Point to Programs, then to Accessories, then to Multimedia.
3. Click CD Player.

COPY TEXT FROM AN ENCYCLOPEDIA TO A WORD PROCESSOR ➤ *pp. 190-191*

1. In Microsoft Encarta, locate the article you want.
2. Highlight the text you want to copy. (If you want the entire article, you don't have to highlight anything.)
3. Point to the downward arrow at the upper-left corner of the article.
4. Choose Copy from the drop-down menu that appears.
5. Select Word Processor from the Tools menu.
6. Use your word processor's Paste command to insert the text into your document.

DAZZLE YOUR FRIENDS AND ASSOCIATES ➤ *pp. 195-197*

A versatile home publishing CD-ROM, like Brøderbund's Print Shop Deluxe Ensemble II, makes it simple to design full-color greeting cards, calendars, banners, business cards, and stationery. You can save time by using the program's ready-made designs, and stylize your documents by choosing from a varied assortment of fonts. You can even embellish your project with clip art, importing images either from the publishing program itself or from a third-party package, such as the Gallery collection from Corel.

TEACH YOUR CHILDREN WELL ➤ *pp. 197-200*

Multimedia software is among the best tools for modern education, especially for young children. Combining interactivity, sound, and cartoon-like graphics, programs such as the Reader Rabbit series make it easy—and fun—for kids even as young as preschool age to learn the basics of reading, writing and 'rithmetic.

Compact discs, also called CDs, first appeared in the early 1980s as a new form of storing music, and within a few years they made the long-playing record obsolete. In the 90s, the CD-ROM—an outgrowth of the CD concept—has spawned the multimedia PC revolution, offering a cornucopia of graphics, animation, video, and sound. Working in tandem with Windows, multimedia software has turned the PC into an interactive tool for business, education, and just plain fun.

definition

CD-ROM: Compact Disc-Read Only Memory. *You can retrieve information from one of these discs, but you can't store anything on it. Exactly like a music CD, which can play music but can't be used to record it.*

MULTIMEDIA MANIA

Chances are, if you bought your PC new within the past couple of years, it's a multimedia system. Multimedia has been the driving force behind home PC sales since 1994, and virtually every PC now being sold in the consumer market is a multimedia model, complete with a CD-ROM drive, a sound card, and stereo speakers. If your PC doesn't support multimedia, don't despair. You can pretty easily upgrade it, assuming that you have the expansion room inside the box, and that your chip is at least a fast 486 (see Chapter 3).

MINIMUM REQUIREMENTS

You go out to buy a new video game for your PC. An action game. An outer space war game. The kids will love it, and you might even sneak in a session yourself when nobody's looking. You look on the bottom of the package, and here's what you see:

- COMPUTER: IBM and 100% compatibles
- OPERATING SYSTEM: Microsoft DOS 6.0 or greater
- CPU: 486/50 minimum required
- VIDEO CARD: 256-color VGA, VLB, or PCI bus recommended for High-Resolution mode
- SOUND CARD: 16-bit, Sound Blaster-compatible
- CD-ROM DRIVE: Double-speed, MPC LEVEL 2 REQUIRED
- MEMORY: 8MB RAM minimum

These are known in the PC industry as *minimum requirements*, sometimes also referred to as *system requirements*. They also represent why many people are terrified of PCs. All the terms and numbers add up to a fancy way of saying that some older PCs may not be able to handle newer programs—particularly programs with a lot of video or computerized action.

Your Main Considerations: Chips and Memory

To get the best performance from today's most complex PC video games, you should have a Pentium processor and 16 megabytes of RAM. But you can usually get along perfectly well with a fast 486 chip—say a 486 DX/50 or better—and 8MB of memory. And even if your chip is a slower 486, and you only have 4 megs of RAM, there are a lot of multimedia programs you'll still be able to run. Educational software, for instance, typically requires less firepower than action-packed games. Consider The Magic School Bus Explores the Ocean, a program from Microsoft that helps young children learn about sea life. With just a 486 SX/25 chip—the slowest 486 of all—and 4 megs of RAM, you and your youngsters can enjoy interactive scenes such as this one:

2×, 4×, 6×, and So on

First there was the single-speed CD-ROM player, followed by double-speed (2×) and quad-speed (4×), which is the current standard. Already, however, 6× and 8× models are on the market. Double-speed players transfer information to your PC twice as fast as single-speed players, quad-speed is twice as fast as double-speed, and so forth. But CD-ROM hardware is well ahead of the software. Most multimedia games are still designed for double-speed CD-ROM drives; in these cases, a faster CD-ROM won't yield much of a performance increase. Still, if you're in the market for a new PC, or if you're upgrading your old one, make sure to get at least a quad-speed CD-ROM drive.

INSTALLING A MULTIMEDIA PROGRAM step by step

In most cases, the best way to install a program from a CD-ROM is the same way you'd install one from a floppy—use Windows 95's Add/Remove Programs tool:

1. Choose Settings from the Start menu.
2. Click Control Panel.
3. Double-click the Add/Remove Programs icon.

4. Click the Install button in the Add/Remove Programs Properties box, and follow the onscreen instructions.

Some CD-ROMs actually initiate the installation process by themselves, when you load a disc for the first time. A lot of multimedia programs by Microsoft now use this technique, which it calls AutoPlay.

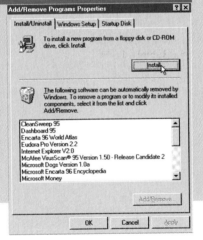

Multimedia and Your Hard Disk

A CD-ROM can hold more than 650MB of information—as much as a fair-sized hard disk, and hundreds of times as much as a floppy. When you install a program from a CD-ROM, only a small portion of it is stored on your hard disk. The rest stays on the CD. When you run the program, the PC accesses the information from the disc as needed. This is why you usually have to put the CD in the drive in order to run the program.

Save Space, Sacrifice Speed

Some multimedia programs, particularly reference works such as encyclopedias, give you installation options. You can store a lot of program data on the hard disk (more than 20 megabytes in some cases), which gives you optimum performance. Or you can choose a slimmer installation, which saves hard disk space but slows the program down when it runs. (Some programs also offer a third "medium" installation option.) If you have plenty of hard disk space, go with full installation.

And You Thought DOS Was Dead!

Although most multimedia programs now being made run in Windows, a small percentage—including many games—still run from DOS. Fortunately, Windows 95 has enough DOS in its innards to accommodate these throwbacks. You can run a DOS session directly from Windows by clicking the Start button, pointing to Programs, and clicking the MS-DOS Prompt icon. This will display a window in which you can run a DOS session, as shown here:

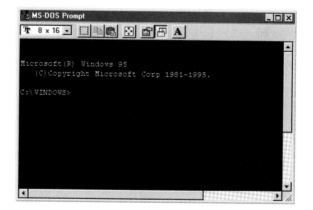

You can have either a small window or a full DOS screen. Press ALT-ENTER to toggle between them.

You also can leave Windows entirely and switch to DOS mode. This is necessary for playing some multimedia games. To run a DOS session in DOS mode:

1. Click the Start button.
2. Choose Shutdown.
3. Click "Restart the computer in MS-DOS mode?".

SHORTCUT

The easiest way to end a DOS session is to type exit *at the DOS prompt. If you're running a DOS window in Windows, this will close the window. In MS-DOS mode, it will restart Windows for you.*

Your Window to Multimedia

Windows 95 gives you some control over how your multimedia software looks and sounds on your system. You can adjust settings for sound volume, the size of video images, and several other things via the Multimedia Properties box, which you can access like this:

1. Click the Start button, point to Settings, and click Control Panel.
2. Double-click the Multimedia icon, which displays the Multimedia Properties box, shown here:

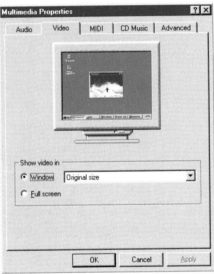

By choosing the tabs at the top of the box, you can modify various settings. In the illustration, for example, you can adjust the size of video images as they will appear on the screen. Bear in mind that the larger the image, the *less* clear it will be.

Let the Music Begin

CD-ROMs and music CDs have a lot in common. They're the same size, hold the same amount of information, and use the same technology. Information is embedded in the discs digitally, and read by a laser in the CD player or CD-ROM drive. You can even play a music CD in your CD-ROM drive. The software that came with your sound card may let you play music CDs, but you also can do it with Windows 95. Here's how:

1. Put a music CD in the CD-ROM player.
2. Make sure your PC speakers are turned on.
3. Sit back and enjoy. Using a feature called AutoPlay, Windows should automatically launch its CD Player and start the music. As it plays, you can work in any other Windows program, such as a word processor or a spreadsheet, as long as it doesn't reside on a CD-ROM.

Just Like a Stereo System

A button for the CD Player appears on the taskbar. By clicking the button, you can display the CD Player, which is shown here:

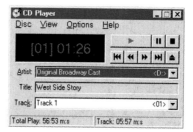

habits & strategies

To adjust the volume for audio CDs, choose Volume Control in the View menu of the CD Player. For optimum results, use this feature in conjunction with the volume knob on your speakers. (But beware! If your teenager finds out about this, you'll find the volume set at full blast.)

You can also start the CD Player manually. Click the Start button and point to Programs, then to Accessories, then to Multimedia, and choose CD Player from the Multimedia menu.

The CD Player gives you many of the same controls you'd find in a regular audio CD player. You can choose which selection to hear, or let the PC play tracks in a random mode. You also can tailor the display to show the time remaining or the time elapsed in a particular selection, or time remaining on the disc.

MULTIMEDIA SOFTWARE

Loosely defined, multimedia is anything that uses a combination of audio and video techniques to convey information. In PC jargon, multimedia is synonymous with CD-ROM technology, mainly because it takes the storage capacity of a compact disc to hold the tons of data necessary for sound and video. CD-ROMs are not just for multimedia, however. Increasingly they are being used as installation disks for all kinds of software programs. For instance, your copy of Windows 95 may be on a CD.

Information, Learning, and Having Fun

Multimedia CD-ROMs can be broken down into three basic categories: reference, education, and entertainment. There are many instances in which these overlap, and in fact the combination of education and entertainment has spawned a hybrid category called *edutainment.* You might even call some programs *edureference* or *refertainment*, but so far nobody has, thank goodness.

REFERENCE PROGRAMS

First, let's take a look at the reference category, which includes encyclopedias, atlases, almanacs, medical guides, and so on. Reference software is ideal for the busy person, since in most cases, it lets you get at information a lot faster than you could if you had to rummage through a book.

Encyclopedias of the Future

One of the dreariest of all school assignments used to be looking something up in an encyclopedia. You had to track down what you wanted using an enormous index, then find it in one of maybe two-dozen volumes, each of which seemed to weigh 50 pounds. Well, those days are gone. CD-ROM encyclopedias are fun to use, giving you sounds, animation, and video, along with text and photos. And you can find what you want in a matter of seconds. Programs such as Microsoft's Encarta and the Grolier Multimedia Encyclopedia have made print encyclopedias an endangered species. One of the best things about a multimedia encyclopedia is that you can easily transfer text, photos, and drawings from the encyclopedia into other applications, such as a word processor. It makes taking notes a cinch.

Copying Text from Encarta 96

1. Highlight the text in the article you'll be copying from. (If you want an entire article, you don't have to highlight anything.)

CAUTION

Hey, students, listen up! Even though you can easily copy something from a CD-ROM encyclopedia, you still have to rewrite it in your own words. Taking credit for something you didn't write is plagiarism. And besides, your teacher's not going to be fooled for a second.

2. Place the mouse pointer on the downward arrow in the upper-left corner of the document. This displays the menu you see here:

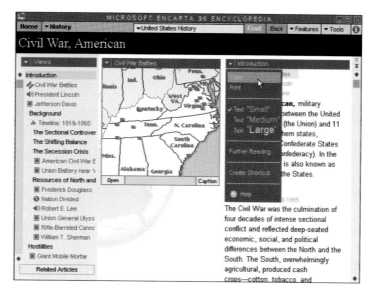

3. Choose Copy, and the text will be copied to Windows' Clipboard.
4. Select Word Processor from Encarta's Tools menu. This will start the word processor that Encarta is using and present you with a blank screen for a new document. (By default, Encarta uses WordPad in Windows 95. However, you can set it up to use any Windows word processor; just select Options from the Information menu, and take it from there.)
5. Choose Paste from the word processor's Edit menu to insert the text into the new document. Or open an existing document, click where you want the text to go, and then choose Paste. The Encarta text will appear in your word processor.

You can use the same routine to copy photos and images into a word processor. The only difference is that the command in the drop-down menu will be Copy Image instead of Copy.

You can also copy images into any program that can use graphics, such as the Microsoft Publisher desktop publishing program. Here's how:

Just because it's multimedia doesn't mean it's better. For example, if you use a dictionary just once in a while, you're better off keeping a printed one at your desk. It's usually faster to look up a word in a book than to wait for a dictionary program to start up on your PC. Similarly, maps in really good printed atlases offer larger, more detailed views than you can get with a software atlas on a PC monitor.

1. Copy the image in Encarta.
2. Start the graphics program (you can keep Encarta open at the same time if you want to), and open the document where you want to put the image.
3. Paste the image into the document.

Atlases, Almanacs, and Other Handy Tools

Because of the speed with which a PC can search through vast amounts of information, the CD-ROM is a perfect vehicle for reference tools. This fact has not been lost on software developers. Among multimedia programs now widely available are atlases, dictionaries, books of quotations, street map finders, and telephone directories. Microsoft even offers a package called Microsoft Bookshelf that includes eight reference volumes—including, of all things, a national ZIP code directory.

Around the World in 80 Seconds

A multimedia atlas is a real treat, offering not only maps, but also nearly boundless information about the four corners of the globe. The World Atlas and Almanac (Version 6) from Mindscape is a good example of the genre:

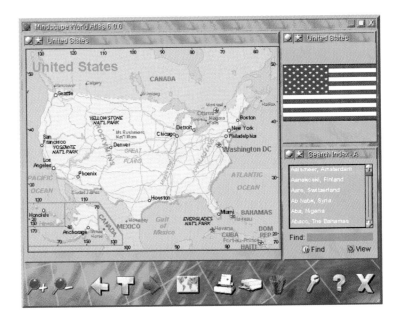

By clicking various place names, you can pull up maps, show flags, play national anthems, and even have the program "speak" the correct pronunciation of a city or country. The program also includes a number of short movies. It's sort of like a travel agency in a computer.

A Boon for Hypochondriacs

Medical reference books have always been best-sellers, and it's no different for multimedia self-help guides. Even the Mayo Clinic has gotten into the act. Used to be, you went to the Mayo Clinic if you had a particularly puzzling condition. Now the respected institution comes to you in the Mayo Clinic Family Health program from IVI Publishing. The program is set up like an interactive medical reference book, including sections on anatomy, diseases, symptoms, and family health. Want to know about the cardiovascular system? The program shows you a detailed schematic, as you can see here, while an authoritative voice explains what you're looking at.

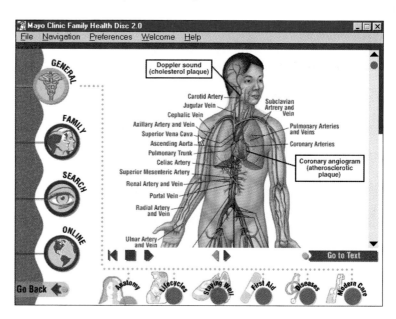

Movies on Demand

One of the most popular multimedia programs is Cinemania from Microsoft. This program—a combination of reference material and entertainment—puts the celluloid history of Hollywood at your finger-tips; it's a must for movie buffs. Cinemania is a searchable, cross-referenced database of movies and movie stars, tapping the power of multimedia to show you still-shots and scenes from top hits over the years, along with snippets of favorite movie tunes. You can even settle bets over who won certain Academy Awards in certain years. Using the Find feature, you can quickly locate information on some 20,000 films—including this one, which most of you will recognize:

Multimedia Reaches a High Note

Reference, education, and entertainment—should we call this "referedutainment"?—all come together in Microsoft's CD-ROMs on great musical composers. So far, the series includes discs on Mozart, Beethoven, Schubert and Strauss. Each release focuses on a single work, attempting to show how it reflects the artist's sensibilities and his times. And they work on several levels. If you're just after a popular history of the composer, you'll get it, in pictures, text, and sound. If you want to delve deeper, each disc provides a fairly scholarly assessment of the featured composition, as in this breakdown of the first movement of Schubert's Trout Quintet:

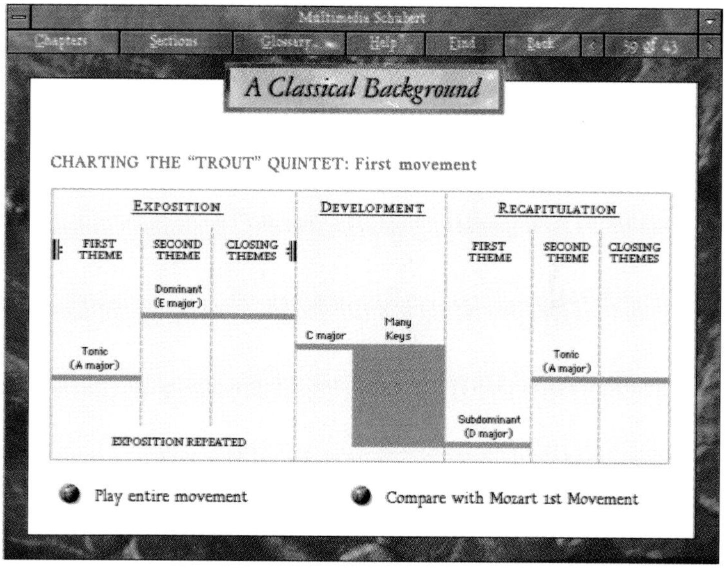

And if you're just in a listening mood, you can instruct the program to simply play the composition. Minimize the program, and you've got some lovely music playing in the background while you go about your other computing chores.

PRODUCTIVITY SOFTWARE

This is a category of multimedia programs that make it easy to perform everyday tasks. One of the best-selling products in this genre is Print Shop from Brøderbund, which comes in a CD-ROM version called Print Shop Deluxe Ensemble II. With this program you can create a variety of fancy items, such as greeting cards, calendars, banners, and business cards, that otherwise would demand a full-fledged desktop publishing program. It can be a real time-saver for a busy person. For instance, suppose you need stationery for your new home business. With Print Shop Deluxe, you can choose from numerous ready-made designs, like the one in the next example:

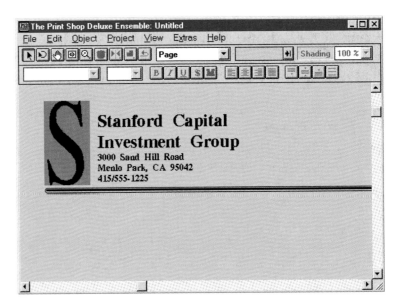

Don't worry; you don't have to change the name of your firm to Stanford Capital Investment Group. The program lets you type in your own name, address, and phone number to replace those used in the template. You can even change the fonts if you don't like the ones in the ready-mades. Print Shop Deluxe comes with an assortment of eye-catching typestyles.

Graphics for Every Occasion

Print Shop Deluxe includes more than 4,000 graphical images. But you also can import graphics from third-party collections of images, which are available on CD-ROMs. These images, called *clip art* or *click art*, can be used in word processing documents, presentations, spreadsheets, etc. A leading purveyor of clip art is Corel, whose Gallery program contains some 10,000 color and black-and-white images of everything from airplanes to holiday symbols. As shown in the following example, you can preview the images in a category—in this case, birds—before selecting the one you want to use in a document:

habits & strategies

To get the most out of a program such as Print Shop Deluxe, you really should have a color printer. The same goes for many educational programs that let kids print out results of their work. FYI, most inkjet printers are now color-capable.

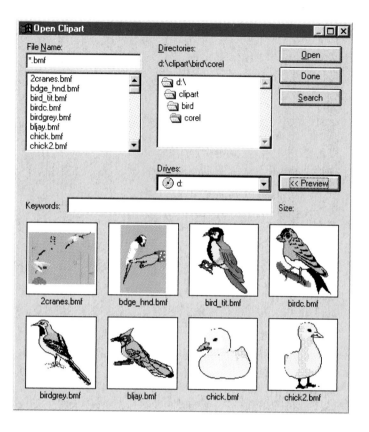

When using a clip art program, you can usually either export an image in a format that your word processor or other program will be able to import. Or you can simply copy the image to Windows' clipboard, and then paste it into your document.

EDUCATIONAL SOFTWARE

Perhaps the greatest impact of multimedia on society so far has been in the area of education. CD-ROMs provide children with enjoyable, effective ways to learn the basics of reading and arithmetic at home (although they're also widely used in the classroom). Older students can study up for college entrance tests. And adults can study such things as foreign languages. For the self-motivated student, this is a wonderful development. No more pencils, no more books, no more teacher's dirty looks. (Except when mom finds out you've been playing Dark Forces instead of being immersed in your algebra program.)

Rabbits, School Buses, and an Elusive International Spy

Some of the most successful educational software comes from an aptly named outfit, The Learning Company. Its chief spokesperson is a character named Reader Rabbit, who has been teaching kids the fundamentals of reading for several years now. In Reader Rabbit's Interactive Reading Journey, kids ages 4 to 7 can learn how to spell and read with the help of the bunny and his pals. (This program is sort of a silicon-based version of Sesame Street.) The following scene, for instance, focuses on words that begin with the letter *s*:

Learning Comes Alive

As technology continues to evolve, software makers are taking advantage of different kinds of multimedia effects. In The Magic School Bus Explores the Ocean, Microsoft has made some of the best use yet of animation to simulate awesome experiences. The bus turns into a submarine (hey, it's magic!), and the teacher, Ms. Frizzle, leads the young PC user through a cartoon exploration of the ocean.

*Many multimedia programs,
such as Carmen Sandiego, take
up the full screen and hide the
Windows taskbar. To access
the taskbar and open the Start
menu, press* CTRL-ESC. *This will
pause the multimedia program,
but you can easily resume it by
pressing its button on the taskbar.*

Mystery Theater, PC-Style

Where in the World is Carmen Sandiego? Well, that's what you're supposed to find out in this venerable best-selling edutainment program from Brøderbund Software. The idea is that as you traipse around the world looking for the elusive master spy, you have to learn about different places in order to track her down. It's basically a geography class disguised as a game. In this scene, for example, you find yourself in Chile:

Your Own Personal Tutor

Multimedia is perfectly suited to teaching language. You can hear the words and sentences you're trying to learn at the same time that you see them displayed on the monitor. A good example of this emerging category of educational software is Learn to Speak Spanish from The Learning Company. In addition to the regular program, you can get an add-on that features speech recognition. With this enhancement, you speak into a microphone that's plugged into the back of your PC, and the program helps you with your pronunciation. The following segment teaches us how to make a hotel reservation:

Learn to Speak Spanish is mainly for those who want to travel south of the border without making fools of themselves. But if you work at it long enough, you might be able to read Gabriel García Márquez in the original—and wouldn't that be a treat?

NOW FOR THE REAL FUN— COMPUTER GAMES!

Reference and education are all well and good, but games are where the action is. Entertainment software is leading the multimedia revolution, using the latest 3-D imagery and virtual reality technology to their fullest. There are action games, mystery/adventure games and even role-playing games, in which the player determines the outcome by his or her choices.

Just Like the Arcade

If it's arcade-like action you're into, what you want is a game that lets you shoot people. Something like Dark Forces from LucasArts, which extends the basic good guys-bad guys theme of the Star Wars movies. Like several other games, including Doom and Descent, Dark Forces employs a simulated 3-D environment that makes you feel as if you can roam anywhere on a space ship to track down the enemy—as shown in the following example:

SHORTCUT

Many entertainment CD-ROMs start out with lengthy introductions, including theme songs and credits—sort of like those in the movies. In many cases you can fast-forward through these opening sequences and get right into the program by clicking the mouse or pressing the spacebar.

You get to choose from different lethal weapons, and the best part is that if you get killed, you can come back to life simply by restarting the game.

Joystick, Mouse, or Keyboard—Which Is Best?

Game companies often recommend that you use a joystick, particularly for games that involve flying action. With a joystick, you can control speed and direction, and at the same time have ready access to your weapons. But you can also use a mouse, or even the keyboard, to operate most games. As it turns out, some kids (they're the experts) prefer using the arrows and other keys on the keyboard, which they think are more precise than a joystick. And some folks just feel more comfortable using a mouse. If you do opt for a joystick, make sure it comes with a connector that matches the game port on your sound card.

Where the Hell Am I?

One of the most successful games in the short history of multimedia is Myst, from Brøderbund. Basically, you're stranded on an island with no idea where you are or what you're doing there. The whole point of the game is to explore the mysterious world by clicking different objects and moving around from scene to scene, unlocking one puzzle after another. This is definitely not a good game for a *really* busy person!

habits & strategies

With some multimedia games, you can type in special codes that give you unlimited ammunition, or that make it impossible to kill you. The game makers themselves don't provide the codes—that would be too simple!—but you can find them in game magazines, and on the Internet.

But if you're trying to relax after a busy day, it can be a treat. The graphics alone are worth the trip:

Getting Into the Part

Another game from Brøderbund, In the 1st Degree, combines scenes of live-action video with role-playing into one of the first interactive multimedia dramas. As the prosecuting attorney, your job is to convict a man of murdering his business partner. You interview witnesses, then go to court, where you are up against a feisty and crafty defense lawyer. If you handle the case right, ferreting out the evidence and getting the truth out of the people on the witness stand, you can get a conviction. Bungle it, though, and the defendant walks. This product epitomizes the trend toward making PC games as realistic as possible:

This Chapter's Going to the Dogs!

Or more precisely, it's ending with the dogs. Proving that anything can turn up on a CD-ROM, you can now go out and spend your money on a program called Microsoft Dogs. This title does not refer to any of Microsoft's less popular software programs (although the ill-fated Bob does come briefly to mind), but rather to man's best friends. Microsoft Dogs includes information on different breeds, along with advice on the care and feeding of the furry set. Or even the unfurry set, such as this Mexican Hairless:

WHAT COULD POSSIBLY BE NEXT???

Defying the old adage that you should never follow a dog act, there are still a few more chapters left in this book. From now on, we'll be dealing with communications software, online services, and the Internet— the *hottest* areas of personal computing. So clear your telephone line, 'cause here we go...

Part 3

WORKING ONLINE

Forget Reagan—The PC is the Great Communicator

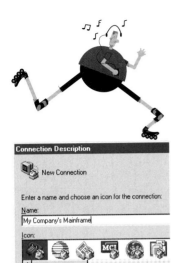

FAST FORWARD

CONNECT TO ANOTHER COMPUTER BY MODEM ➤ *pp. 213-216*

1. Click the Start button and point to Programs, then to Accessories.
2. Click HyperTerminal, then double-click the Hypertrm.exe icon to open the HyperTerminal program.
3. Follow the instructions to create a connection file for the computer you want to reach.
4. In the Connect box, click Dial. When the connection is complete, sign onto the other computer or service.

TAKE OVER ANOTHER PC ➤ *pp. 216-218*

1. Make sure your remote access program (LapLink, for instance) is loaded and running, both on your PC and on the one you want to gain access to. The remote PC can be anywhere in the world, as long as you can reach it via telephone.
2. Dial the remote PC and wait for the connection. If you're using LapLink, you'll see directories of both computers appear side by side on your screen. You can then transfer files from one machine to the other by dragging them to different folders.

GO ONLINE, BIG-TIME ➤ *pp. 218-219*

(If you don't, the last two chapters of this book are liable to be pretty dull reading.)

1. Get a software disk for the online service you'd like to try. America Online, CompuServe, and Prodigy all give away their software for free, and will even give you a free trial period online.
2. Load the software, and then follow the instructions to register for the service online. Keep your credit card handy. Services bill by the month, and the payment goes on your plastic.

CONSIDER AN INTERNET PROVIDER ➤ *pp. 220-222*

You can surf the Net via one of the online services like AOL, but if you spend a lot of time in cyberspace, it's going to cost you. A cheaper alternative is an Internet Service Provider. The main things to look for are:

1. A provider with an access phone number near you, so you don't end up paying toll charges.
2. One that charges no more than $20 per month to use the Net.

TURN YOUR PC INTO A FAX MACHINE ➤ *pp. 222-228*

Using a program like Microsoft Fax, you can fax a document directly from a Windows program, such as Word for Windows 95. Here's how:

1. With the document open and ready to go, choose Print from the File menu.
2. Choose Microsoft Fax from the drop-down list of printers available on your system.
3. Click OK. The Fax program takes over, guiding you through the process of sending the fax.

Most historians will say that the PC age began in 1976, when Steve Jobs and Steve Wozniak built the first Apple computer in Jobs' garage. That may be true, but the most visionary idea actually was voiced in the 1967 film *Cool Hand Luke,* when the prison camp captain leaned over a defiant Paul Newman and uttered the famous line, "What we got here is a failure to communicate." For most of the past two decades, the PC industry has been grappling with the problems of communication—how to make computers talk to each other. Lucky for us, many of the difficulties have now been ironed out. Communications software has evolved from being ridiculously complicated to being quite simple and, to use the overtaxed phrase, user-friendly. As you'll see in this chapter, you can now log onto a mainframe, control one PC from another one, send a fax, and tap into the Internet without an advanced degree in computer science.

FIRST THINGS FIRST— THE MODEM

If your PC already has Windows 95 and a modem, chances are you're all set up for online communications. To see how your modem is configured, do the following:

1. Click the Start button and point to Settings, then click Control Panel.
2. Double-click the Modems icon to display the Modems Properties dialog box, which will show you what kind of modem you have.

3. Click the Properties button to display the properties for your particular modem, as shown here:

This box contains such information as which port the modem is running on and its current maximum speed; both of these are settings you can change.

Terms that Hopefully You'll Never Have to Deal with

As PC communications become more and more standardized, there is less and less need to fool around with modem settings. As long as the computers at both ends of a connection use the same settings, you're not likely to have a problem. The following settings need to match:

Data Bits The number of bits that represent a single character of data, usually 8 or 7.

Parity A method of checking for errors during transmissions. Parity terms include None, Even and Odd.

Stop Bit A bit that tells a receiving computer when pieces of a transmission end. Most modems are set for 1 or 2 stop bits.

If You Must Change Modem Settings

These days, most modems call for 8 data bits, no parity and 1 stop bit; this combination is commonly referred to as 8-N-1. This is the Windows 95 default, and it's becoming widely accepted throughout the industry. However, if you find yourself staring at garble when you log onto another computer, you may have to change one or more of these settings. (Some older modems, for instance, prefer 7-E-1.) To make any changes, do this:

1. Display the Properties box for your modem, using the three steps listed earlier.
2. Click the Connection tab to display the current settings, which Windows calls Connection Preferences. Use the drop-down lists, shown here, to make any necessary changes.

Take heart. Once you set up your modem, Windows will automatically apply the settings to any software program that uses a modem (as long as the program is designed for Windows 95). The only thing you'll probably have to set will be the number you want to dial.

Location, Location, Location

To facilitate automatic dialing, Windows lets you set up "locations," which tell the modem where your PC is at the time the call is being made. This way, Windows knows if you're dialing long-distance, and will automatically add the area code and perhaps a *1* to the number. You can set up multiple locations, which means that you can store information about your home and your office, as well as branch offices, hotels you stay at regularly, or other locations where you often have to use your modem. (Obviously, this feature is most useful for people with notebook computers who do a lot of traveling.) Here's how to set up a location:

1. Click the Start button and point to Settings, then click Control Panel.
2. Double-click the Modems icon to display the Modems Properties dialog box.

3. Click the Dialing Properties button, and fill in the appropriate spaces in the box you see here:

Dialing Properties

My Locations

Where I am:

I am dialing from: Default Location   New...   Remove

The area code is: 707

I am in: United States of America (1)

How I dial from this location:

To access an outside line, first dial: ☐ for local, ☐ for long distance.

☐ Dial using Calling Card: Change...

☑ This location has call waiting. To disable it, dial:

The phone system at this location uses: ⦿ Tone dialing ○ Pulse dialing

COMMUNICATIONS SOFTWARE

In pre-Windows days, communications programs were used for nearly every computer-to-computer connection over a phone line. But today, most online services and Internet access providers have their own graphical, easy-to-use software. Basic communications programs play a smaller role than they used to, but they still come in handy. You can use them to access electronic bulletin boards and some e-mail accounts, and to connect your PC by modem to another computer system—perhaps even the mainframe at your office.

HyperTerminal Won't Make You Hyperventilate

Windows 95 comes with a built-in communications tool called HyperTerminal. Actually, it's not "hyper" anything, but rather a no-frills program that lets you easily connect to another computer via modem. Assuming you have your modem configured and ready to go, HyperTerminal will walk you through the process of setting up a connnection. Here's how it goes:

1. Start HyperTerminal by doing the following: Click the Start button, point to Programs and then Accessories, and then

click HyperTerminal. In the HyperTerminal folder, double-click the Hypertrm.exe icon.

2. Type in a name for your connection, such as **Company Computer**, and pick an icon to represent it. Then click OK. This brings up the Phone Number dialog box.

3. Enter the number of the computer you want to call, and click OK. This brings up the Connect box:

If there's a particular number you connect to all the time, create a Windows Shortcut for it and put it on the Start menu or the desktop. (See Chapter 4 for instructions on creating a Shortcut.) That way, you won't have to keep going to the HyperTerminal folder to make your connection.

4. Click Dial to start the connection.

5. When the connection is made, you'll probably have to enter a user name and a password before the computer you're calling will let you in. This is a standard security procedure. If you want to access your company's computer, and you don't know how, you'll have to ask one of the computer magicians at work how to sign onto the system.

To end the session, type in any necessary log-off sequence, then click the Disconnect button on the HyperTerminal toolbar, as shown here, to end the phone call.

When you close HyperTerminal after creating a connection, you'll be prompted to save it. Once you've done that, you can use the connection by double-clicking its icon in the HyperTerminal folder.

Saving Text from an Online Session

There are two ways to save text that appears on your monitor during an online session. You can copy it, just as you would in any Windows program, and paste it into another program, like a word processor. Or you can capture it in a file of its own as it comes in. To accomplish the latter, click Capture Text in the Transfer menu. The following dialog box appears:

Capture Text	? ☒
Folder:	C:\Program Files\Accessories\HyperTerminal
File:	cessories\HyperTerminal\CAPTURE.TXT	Browse...
	Start	Cancel

Give the file a name, then press Start. From this point on, anything that is displayed on the screen will be stored in the file. To stop the capture, revisit the Capture Text menu option, which now includes a submenu with Cancel and Pause options.

Sending and Receiving Files

HyperTerminal also can be used to send and receive actual files, including ASCII files and binary files—which contain programs or images. To ensure fast, error-free transfer of binary files, you need to use a binary transmission *protocol*. Common protocols include Xmodem, Ymodem, and Zmodem. Zmodem is considered one of the most efficient protocols, and is the default for Windows 95. However, you can pick another one at the time you initiate the transfer using the Transfer menu. It doesn't much matter which protocol you use, as long as the other computer also is using it (and, of course, it has to be turned on with its communications software running).

Want More Bells and Whistles?

If HyperTerminal is a little too bare-bones for your tastes, there are other options. You can go for a full-fledged communications program like the best-selling ProComm Plus for Windows, which has every option imaginable. Another alternative is the communications program that comes with Microsoft Works for Windows 95. This integrated suite was discussed in Chapter 6 as an inexpensive package featuring a

definition

protocol: The forms of ceremony observed by diplomats and heads of states. Also, procedures governing transmission of data between computers. How did those two definitions find their way into the same word? Probably because they both involve tedious routines that may seem needlessly time-consuming, but are actually quite important for smoothing the way to successful communication.

serviceable word processor, database, and spreadsheet. Well, the communications program is pretty good too.

Logging On Made Easy

Communications programs have never been very good at automating the process of signing onto another computer system. Many programs make you go through hoops to create an automatic sign-on procedure, and some, like HyperTerminal, can't even generate one. This means that you have to type in your user ID and password each time you connect. But Works for Windows makes creating a sign-on script as simple as a couple of clicks of the mouse. In fact, the online help explains the procedure so well, it doesn't pay to say it another way. Here's how it goes:

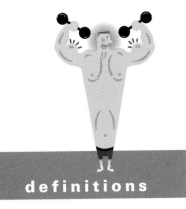

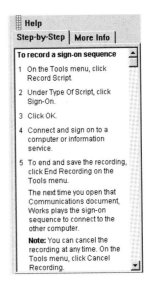

definitions

network: *A group of computers linked together and sharing resources such as programs, data lines, and printers.*

server: *The computer at the center of a network. The server can be a powerful PC, a workstation, or a larger computer. It holds the operating system for the whole network. Large companies can have many servers, each handling a portion of the overall corporate network.*

THE DIRECT CONNECTION

With the rapid growth in the popularity of mobile computing, busy people are relying increasingly on direct connections, linking their home PCs and notebooks with their PCs and *networks* at the office. Thanks to a new generation of software, you can control a computer anywhere in the world over a phone line. You can manipulate folders and files on the remote PC, work with documents, and even use the printer connected to the PC. If you didn't mind paying for the call, you could even

CAUTION

Using remote access, a person could, either inadvertently or deliberately, alter or delete crucial files on your PC or network. Fortunately, remote access programs include security provisions to prevent unwanted intrusions by those who shouldn't be messing about in your system. Bottom line—remote access makes you vulnerable, so be careful.

use a computer thousands of miles away from a notebook in a plane. Now *that's* impressive.

Like Taking Over Someone's Soul

Leading programs for remote access include Traveling Software's LapLink, and Norton's PC Anywhere. For the process to work, both computers must be running the same remote control program. The PC initiating the call is the "guest," while the one that's being controlled is the "host." Kind of a high-tech version of "The Body Snatchers." Using LapLink, once you establish a connection, your notebook or PC displays a split screen that lists the folders and files on both your machine and the remote one, as shown here:

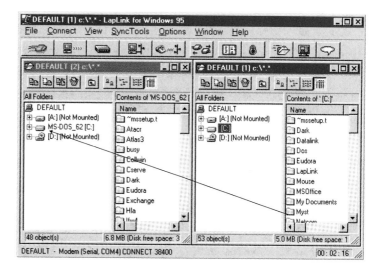

To copy files from one PC to the other, you drag them from one folder to another.

Before you run out and buy a fancy laptop PC for remote access computing, have a chat with your company's systems guru. There may be technical barriers, such as security "firewalls," that could make remote access more trouble than it's worth.

You Are Now Under My Control

Now comes the real fun part. Click the Open Remote Control Window icon on LapLink's toolbar, and your PC displays the screen of the remote PC in a Window. Whatever is on the other PC's desktop appears on yours, in exactly the same position. You can start programs and work with files—even change the look of the desktop itself.

Now That's What You Call Networking! Yet another good tool for remote computing is the Dial-Up Networking feature in Windows 95. It lets you connect to your company's network through a remote access server, which means you can do things like read and send office e-mail from home or when you're on the road. By combining Dial-Up Networking with LapLink, you can gain access to other PCs on the network that also are running LapLink. Nifty!

A Question of Speed (or Lack Thereof)

No matter what sort of online computing you do—data communications, remote access, or surfing the Internet—you're going to be frustrated by how long it takes over a regular phone line. The fact is that we're still in the stone age when it comes to data transmission. At 28.8 kbps, modems are reaching the limit of what they can do over conventional telephone lines...but help is on the way.

ISDN At Your Service

ISDN, which can work up to four times as fast as the fastest regular modem, is already available to residents in most parts of the nation through local telephone companies. Because it is digital technology, ISDN (for *I*ntegrated *S*ervices *D*igital *N*etwork) requires a special adapter, also called an ISDN modem. These are available from companies such as 3Com and Motorola; they're more expensive than regular modems— between $200 and $300—but the price should come down as ISDN usage becomes more widespread.

GOING ONLINE

The biggest rage in computing these days is going online. Your PC isn't just an isolated machine anymore—it's your window to a world that is growing smaller by the day. Through a commercial online service such as America Online, you can keep up with news, weather, sports, and entertainment, while the Internet lets you connect to universities, businesses, and government organizations all over the globe. Subsequent chapters will deal with online services and the Internet in-depth, but this seems like a good place to discuss how to actually get connected.

habits & strategies

To get ISDN service, you need to have a special line connected to your house. The service also costs more than regular phone service—around $25 a month plus charges for connect time. (The rates vary from state to state.) Before you take the plunge, research the costs to make sure it's worth your while. Generally, ISDN is best suited for people who do a lot of work online.

218

Three of the Big Four online

services—AOL, CompuServe,

and Prodigy—offer free trials.

(Microsoft does not.) So if you

can't decide which service

is best for you, why not try

more than one? It's a no-lose

proposition. Just don't sign up

and then forget about it, or else

you'll find yourself paying for

something you're not using.

Computer Degree Not Required

With a commercial online service like America Online, CompuServe, Prodigy, or the Microsoft Network, going online is as easy as taking out your credit card. Here's all you have to do:

1. Get ahold of the software for the online service you want. This should be no problem. Most of the services give Windows-compatible access software away at every opportunity, just to lure new customers. AOL disks are packaged with magazines, and CompuServe sends its software through the mail. There must be 10 million of these disks floating around. And software for the Microsoft Network comes on every new PC that has Windows 95.

2. Load the software, then follow the instructions to set it up and to sign up for the service online.

Pick a Number

During the online registration process, you will be asked to choose an access number and an alternate number from a list of numbers in your area. You'll also have to provide some information, including the speed of your modem. You can always change these settings later. In CompuServe, for example, you do it by clicking the Session Settings option on the Special menu, then entering your new settings in this window:

Setup Session Settings	
Session	
Current: CIS Connection	New Delete
Alternate: [None] Connector: COM4:	
Name: David C. Einstein Baud Rate: 38400	
User ID: 103522,612 Network: CompuServe	
Password: ******** Dial Type: Tone	
Access Phone: 14154445200 ☒ Use Winsock Configure	

OK More... Modem... LAN... Cancel Help

CHOOSING AN ON-RAMP
TO THE SUPERHIGHWAY

There are three main ways to connect to the Internet:

- Via a major online service, such as America Online, CompuServe, or Prodigy. You can connect to the Net directly from these services, so you don't need any special software. But using an online service to surf the Net can get expensive if you spend too much time in cyberspace.
- Through an Internet Service Provider, such as Netcom Online Communications. This is the cheapest solution if you plan to spend a lot of time on the Net. Accounts cost an average of $20 a month for unlimited usage.
- Through your office PC, if it's on a network that includes Internet access. This is the fastest approach, since network connections are generally much faster than modems.

Special Software for the Net

You can't use just any communications program to connect your PC to the Internet. You need software that incorporates *TCP/IP* and *Winsock;* these features are lacking in programs like HyperTerminal. They are available, however, in software specifically designed for using the Net, which we'll discuss in detail in Chapter 12. The Internet Jumpstart Kit included in the Microsoft Plus! accessory pack for Windows 95 contains Internet access software. And many other Internet service providers offer free software for accessing their services—the Netcruiser program from Netcom, for example.

Going Through an Internet Provider

If you want to use an Internet service provider, find one that has an access number in your vicinity so you don't end up paying for a toll call each time you log on. Then call the provider, who will either sign you up over the phone, or send you an access software program so you can register online.

definitions

TCP/IP: A communications protocol for linking different kinds of computers in a network. It's the standard protocol for the Internet.

Winsock: An interface that allows Windows to work with TCP/IP.

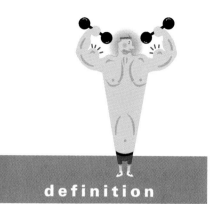

definition

PPP: Point to Point Protocol. *(Just what you needed, another protocol.) This one is a standard for connecting a PC to the Internet via a direct dial-up connection. It is replacing an earlier protocol called SLIP (Serial Line Internet Protocol).*

Setting Up a Connection

Let's use the Microsoft Internet Jumpstart Kit to illustrate the process of getting onto the Internet. This software lets you connect your PC to the Net in a number of ways. You can go through the Microsoft Network or any other Internet service provider that has a *PPP* connection. The Internet Setup Wizard will guide you through the process. The Wizard appears when you first load the Internet Jumpstart Kit, but you can call it up anytime by doing the following:

1. Click the Start button, and point to Programs, then to Accessories.
2. Point to Internet Tools and click Internet Setup Wizard. If you click Help, you'll get a brief description of your options:

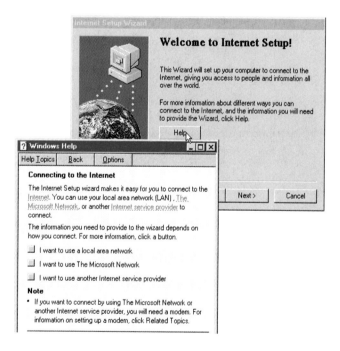

Get a Pencil to Jot Down Some Numbers If you're connecting to an Internet service provider through somebody else's software—Microsoft's for instance—you'll need to get some specific information from your provider to use in setting up the connection. Be sure to find out the following information:

habits & strategies

Save yourself some time by taking a trial run through the Internet Setup Wizard. Jot down the prompts for the information you don't have. Then exit from the Wizard, and call your Internet service provider to get the missing information. After that, you can use the Wizard for real and set up your connection.

- The Internet access phone number. (Remember, try to find one near you to avoid those toll charges.)
- Your user name and password.
- The Internet Protocol (IP) address. Every computer on the Internet has an IP address. If you have a standard access plan (the $20-a-month kind), your service provider automatically assigns an IP address to you that may be different each time you sign on. Bottom line is, you don't have to worry about it.
- The address of the Domain Name Service (DNS) server. This is a series of numbers separated by periods that identifies the server hosting your Internet session. Your service provider should be able to supply you with a DNS address and at least one alternative that your PC can use if the first server can't be reached. In the Internet Setup Wizard, the entry box for DNS numbers looks like this:

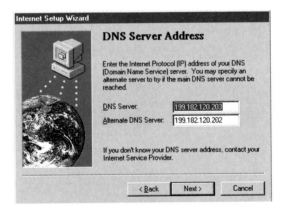

USING YOUR PC AS A FAX MACHINE

Virtually all modems now being sold can handle faxes as well as voice communications. If you're a busy person, chances are good that you have to send a lot of faxes, and receive a lot as well. Why not turn your PC into a virtual fax machine? There are compelling reasons to try it:

- It's cheaper than shelling out hundreds of dollars for a fax machine.
- You won't get a stack of incoming faxes on your desk, because you can view them on your monitor and print them out only if you want to.
- You can easily keep logs of the faxes you've sent and received, and store the faxes themselves in your PC. And you can discard them just as you would any file—with a click or two of the mouse.
- Faxing by PC is a small but important step in helping the environment by conserving paper.

Nothing but the Fax (Software)

Assuming you have a modem and a phone line, all you need is fax software. There are a few really good programs out there—in particular, the top-selling WinFax Pro from Delrina/Symantec. Some fancy communications programs, like ProComm Plus for Windows, include faxing capabilities. And Windows 95 comes with a nifty fax program of its own called Microsoft Fax.

Faxing with Microsoft

To use Microsoft Fax, you'll also need Microsoft Exchange, the program Windows 95 user to manage electronic messaging, including e-mail and faxes. Microsoft Exchange and Microsoft Fax may or may not have been installed when Windows 95 was first loaded onto your PC. To find out if they were, do the following:

1. Click the Start button, point to Settings and click Control Panel.
2. Double click Add/Remove Programs.
3. Click the Windows Setup tab. This will show you which Windows 95 components are installed, as in the following example:

CAUTION

Microsoft Exchange eats up memory like the eggplant that ate Chicago. It will run in 8 megabytes of RAM, but you'll need at least 16 if you're short on patience.

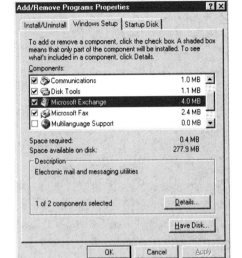

4. Look at the checkboxes next to Microsoft Exchange and Microsoft Fax. If there are checkmarks in both boxes, and the boxes are white, you're in business; skip to step 5. If either box is checked but is gray, only a portion of the program has been installed. (Click Details to find out which part or parts are missing.) If a box is empty, no part of the program has been installed. To install it now, click its box so that a checkmark appears.

5. Click OK or press ENTER, either to exit from the Add/Remove Programs Properties box or to start the installation process. (If you're installing Microsoft Exchange or Microsoft Fax, have your Windows 95 CD-ROM or floppy disks handy; you'll need them.)

First, You Gotta Set Things Up

Before you start faxing everybody from your PC to show them how computer literate you are, you've got to set up the Microsoft Fax software. Here's how it's done:

1. Open the Microsoft Exchange window, shown in the following example.

SHORTCUT

Top-notch fax programs such as Microsoft Fax and WinFax Pro let you create address books for names and numbers of people who you often send faxes to. This can be a real time saver—just the ticket for a really busy person.

Just in case you're wondering, you don't have to let the program know where it's dialing from. Remember? You already entered that information in the Dialing Properties box when you first set up your modem! So when you fax something long distance, the Microsoft Fax program should automatically add the area code, along with a 1 if necessary.

You can do this either by clicking the Start button, pointing to Programs, and clicking Microsoft Exchange (pretty simple), or by double-clicking the Inbox icon on your desktop (even simpler).

2. Okay, now choose Microsoft Fax Tools from the Tools menu.

3. Click Options to bring up the Microsoft Fax Properties box. This is where you choose default settings for the fax program.

4. Click the tabs at the top of the box to see the various options. The Message tab, for instance, lets you automatically include a cover page with each fax. The User tab displays the following box, where you put information about yourself that goes on the cover letter:

After the Setup, Sending Is Easy

You can send a fax from Microsoft Fax, WinFax Pro or almost any other fax program directly from another program, such as a word processor.

FAXING FROM WORD FOR WINDOWS step by step

1. Open the document you want to fax.
2. Choose Print from the File menu.
3. Open the drop-down list of printers that are set up on your system, and select Microsoft Fax.
4. Click OK. The Microsoft Fax program prompts you to enter the name and fax number of your recipient, plus any message you want to include on the cover letter.
5. When you're all done, hit Finish, and the fax goes on its merry way.

When You're on the Receiving End

Receiving a fax can be even easier than sending one. The fax program has to be running (and in Microsoft's case, the Microsoft Exchange program has to be running). But with most fax programs you can select automatic reception mode, then minimize the program so that it just appears as a button on the taskbar. Then whenever a fax comes in, the program will alert you with a status box, like this one from WinFax Pro:

Once a Fax has been received, you can view it or print it. In WinFax Pro you can even edit it, using OCR (that's *Optical Character Recognition*). OCR technology lets you edit a faxed (or scanned) document just as if it had been created in a word processor. Which is cool, because normally your PC treats such documents as pictures, and you can't edit them. With WinFax, you can save the text of a fax to the Windows Clipboard and paste it into a Microsoft Word document, for example, or save it as a text file. To edit a plain old, garden variety fax with no graphics, do the following:

1. Open WinFax Pro's Viewer.
2. Open the fax.
3. Choose OCR from the Setup menu to display the OCR Properties box.
4. Click the After Recognition tab, which displays the box you see here:

5. Choose an editing option. You can edit the fax before saving it (Interactive text edit), send it to the Windows Clipboard, or save it as a text file and work with it later.

The Downside—or What's My Line?

A lot of folks are nervous about receiving faxes on their PCs, especially if they only have one telephone line that has to share faxes and phone calls. Some fax programs help out by alerting you if an incoming call is actually somebody who wants to talk to you, rather than a fax message. And you can always disable automatic reception; that way, you can

If you want to use your PC to

receive faxes on a regular basis,

your best bet by far is to get

a second phone line. This

approach offers an additional

bonus, because you can use the

second line for the Internet and

other online stuff, and you won't

be tying up the family phone line

in the process.

answer the phone like you normally would. Here's how to receive a fax manually with WinFax Pro:

1. Whenever you answer the phone and hear a beep indicating an incoming fax, start WinFax, if it's not already active.
2. Choose Manual Receive Now from the Receive menu. (If you're running WinFax in a minimized mode, right-click the WinFax button on the taskbar and choose Manual Receive Now from the shortcut menu.)
3. When you hear your modem pick up the line, and "Answering" appears on the WinFax Status dialog box, hang up the phone's handset immediately. WinFax will then receive the fax.

WHAT'S LEFT?

Two more chapters, that's what. And these may be the most enjoyable of all, because they give you more details about the hottest thing in computing—going online. In the following chapter, you'll learn more about the commercial online services, including America Online, CompuServe, Prodigy, and the Microsoft Network—so make sure your modem is up and running.

News, Weather, Sports, Entertainment— It's All Online

FAST FORWARD

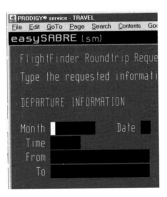

GET AROUND QUICKLY ➤ *pp. 235-236*

Finding what you want on an online service can be tricky and time-consuming. To cut to the chase, use the Go function in CompuServe, the Go to Keyword feature in America Online, or the Jump To feature in Prodigy. Type in the topic you're looking for, and the service will beam you directly to it.

CHECK THE WEATHER ➤ *pp. 237-238*

Before you pack for that next ski trip, get online and check out the conditions on the slopes. Here's how to do it using Prodigy:
1. Choose Jump To from the GoTo menu.
2. Type in **weather** and press ENTER.
3. Double-click Ski Conditions.
4. Click West to display conditions for major resorts in the West.

BE YOUR OWN TRAVEL AGENT ➤ *pp. 240-241*

Using the easySABRE airline reservations system on AOL, CompuServe or Prodigy, you can find the best deals on air fares and reserve your ticket. To find flight information, including prices, using Prodigy:
1. Click Travel on the main menu.
2. Choose easySABRE Main Menu.
3. Click Reservations and type in your password. (If you're not already an easySABRE member, you can sign up for the free service now.)
4. Click easySABRE Reservations Menu.
5. Select FlightFinder, and follow the instructions.

GET A STOCK QUOTE ➤ *pp. 241-242*

To check the price of a company's stock through CompuServe:

1. Click the Quotes button on the toolbar.
2. Click Add and type in the stock's ticker symbol, which adds it to your online portfolio.
3. Click Get to see the latest action on the stock.

DOWNLOAD SOFTWARE ➤ *pp. 244-145*

To download a software file through AOL:

1. Click the File Search button on the toolbar.
2. Select the category or categories that you want to search.
3. Click the List Matching Files button.
4. If you find something you want, click the Download Now button.

SEND SOMEONE E-MAIL ➤ *pp. 245-250*

Call up your online service's e-mail feature. They all look more or less the same. Fill in the Internet address of the person you want to reach, the subject of the message, and the message itself. Then send it on its way. (You can set online services to alert you when *you* have new incoming e-mail.)

What if you could use your PC to catch up on your favorite sport? Or make plane reservations for your trip to Boston, and then check on the weather there right before you leave? Or keep up-to-date on how your stocks are doing? Or correspond with your best friend, who lives in Florida? Well, you can do all of this and more using a commercial online service. Thanks to today's speedy modems, Windows-based navigation software, and inexpensive membership rates, online companies are enjoying a gold rush of popularity. Along with the Internet, they represent the confluence of communication and computing that is definitely the wave of the future.

THE BIG FOUR

Today there are four major commercial online services: America Online (AOL), CompuServe, Prodigy, and the Microsoft Network (MSN). Each offers unique content and its own flavor of interface, but all the services share the same basic features. They give you news, weather, sports, entertainment, and investment services. And they all charge monthly subscription fees. CompuServe is the oldest of the services, and offers the most information. AOL, with its slick interface, now has the most members of any online service. Prodigy still seems to be maneuvering for its place in the sun. And MSN, the newest entry, is growing fast—Microsoft had signed up a million members barely six months after the service went live in August of 1995.

What You Get for Ten Bucks a Month...

As of early 1996, AOL, CompuServe and Prodigy all charge $9.95 a month for up to five hours of use. Anything over that will cost you $2.95 an hour. The Microsoft Network is $4.95 a month, which includes three hours, and $2.50 for each additional hour. You also can get more

habits & strategies

Most online services now offer access at 28.8 kbps, which is the fastest speed attainable with today's fastest modems and standard telephone lines. Make sure to connect to your service at the highest speed possible, or you'll spend time (and money) just waiting for graphics to appear on your monitor.

CAUTION

If you have Call Waiting active on your telephone, an incoming call will bomb you out of an online session. The good news is, you can set up your modem so that Call Waiting is disabled whenever you're online. Double-click the Modems icon on the Windows 95 Control Panel, click Dialing Properties, and then enter the information necessary to disable Call Waiting. In most cases, it's *70. If you're not sure, ask your phone company.

expensive plans that include more time, in case you want to use an online service as your gateway to the Internet.

...And What You Don't Get

America Online's basic service charge covers almost everything that AOL offers. The other online companies, however, offer services for which they charge extra. CompuServe, for instance, has the industry's best stable of financial and investment resources, but you can pay dearly for something like a Wall Street research report. Fortunately, the online services always let you know when you're straying into territory that will cost you extra.

WELCOME!

Assuming you've loaded the service's software into your PC and opened an account (see Chapter 10), you'll see a basic menu each time you sign on. From here you'll have point-and-click access to different areas of interest, including news, sports, travel, and entertainment. CompuServe's main screen looks like this:

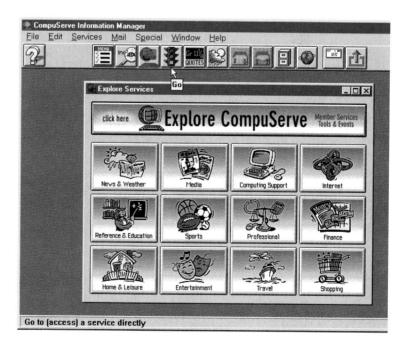

Finding Your Way Around

Online services are more complicated than other Windows programs. In addition to the familiar menus and toolbars, the windows themselves are gateways to more windows—and it's a lot of work to go through two or three windows just to get to a weather report or a sports score. Fortunately, there are easier ways. On the CompuServe toolbar, you'll notice an icon marked Go. Click this icon and type in a topic, and CompuServe will take you directly there. AOL and Prodigy have similar features to help you bypass menus and layers of windows. In Prodigy, choose Jump To from the GoTo menu (or press CTRL-J). In AOL, click the Go to Keyword icon, which brings up this dialog box:

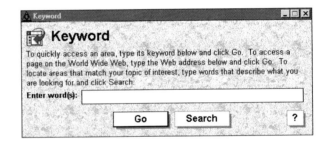

CONTENT IS KING

Online services are no different than television in one sense: content is king. The more information a service offers, the better it can compete. As a result, the major services have waged a never-ending battle, all vying to outdo each other with more online newspapers, magazines, entertainment features, investment advice, reference materials, and anything else they can cram in. It's a wonderful example of how competition can improve things.

A Newsstand Inside Your PC

Online services don't provide much content themselves. Most of it comes from outside venders, such as news agencies, magazine publishers, and broadcasters. For example, CompuServe offers online editions of *Fortune, Sports Illustrated,* and *New York* magazine, among others, while AOL's list includes *Business Week, Consumer Reports,* and *Atlantic Monthly.* Each service offers dozens of titles, including entertainment and computer publications.

This Just In...

There isn't much difference between the news from different online services. Most of it comes from one of the big news organizations, such as the Associated Press or Reuters. It's updated at regular intervals throughout the day—an advantage over the daily newspaper.

You might ask why anyone would turn to a PC for news when we get bombarded by it every day through newspapers, radio, and TV. The answer is the ease with which online services let you access stories you want, while skipping news that doesn't interest you. AOL is a good example. Click Today's News on the main menu, and you get the window shown here, which features a list of top news items, as well as buttons for accessing other news areas.

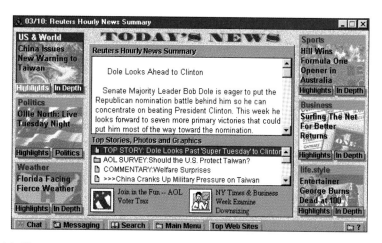

It's like a newspaper, but finding stuff in it is a lot easier. Also, you don't get ink on your fingers.

How's the Weather Out There?

Having an online service is sort of like having a TV weatherman in your PC (now there's a disgusting thought). You can get updated forecasts and temperature maps for any place you're likely to be heading. Also, it's nice to know there's snow on the ground *before* booking that expensive ski trip. Here's how you'd use Prodigy to get up-to-date ski conditions:

1. Choose Jump To from the GoTo menu. Type in **weather** and press ENTER. A list of options appears, including Regional Weather, US City Weather and Weather Maps.
2. Double-click Ski Conditions.
3. Click West, which displays the following window. (Looks like a grand time to hit the slopes!)

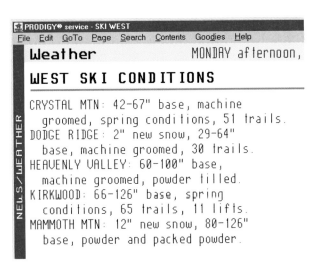

Sports Nuts Rejoice!

When it comes to sports news, online services really shine. They combine hard news with analysis, statistics, and feature material in a format you could never get in a newspaper or on TV. In fact, ESPN, the sports network, understands full well the potential of online sports. Not only does it have its own Internet service, it also provides information for Prodigy. Speaking of which, I *just* checked Prodigy for pro basketball scores and got the following screen:

**habits &
strategies**

*Later in this chapter, you'll learn
how to* download *printed
information, such as news and
magazine articles, from your
online service into your PC.
Downloading is a good idea if an
article is very long, because
every minute you're online is
charged to your account. A
word of warning, however:
Unless you get the proper
permission, you can't use
material from an online service
for commercial purposes. It's all
covered by copyrights.*

You'll notice that as I write this, most of the day's games haven't started yet. But if I weren't so busy writing, I could get the starting lineups for the ones that are about to begin, and see the final scores for games already completed—plus partial scores for those in progress. (Notice also that the Bulls just beat the Pacers—no surprise there.)

That's Entertainment?

Online services do the best they can to cover movies and television, but the limitations on transmitting graphical material over a phone line really hurt. This is one area where the PC still has a long way to go. You're really better off reading online entertainment magazines, checking out movie reviews, and doing other things that really don't require a PC. True Hollywood buffs never seem to get enough of this stuff, however, and there are some cute features aimed right at them. AOL has something called Follywood that offers a refreshing, not-too-serious approach to the movie business—kind of like a PC version of *Entertainment Tonight*. It even includes contests where you can win free time on AOL. The main window for Follywood changes along with the movie scene. Here's a recent example:

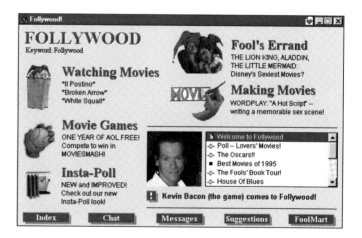

GATEWAY TO FAR-OFF PLACES

One of the most useful aspects of online services is the way they can help you plan and arrange for travel. Whether you're looking for a good hotel in London or a bed & breakfast in Canada, you can use your PC to find the right accommodations and make arrangements for your trip.

Who Needs a Travel Agent?

Using the airline reservation system easySABRE, which is available at no charge on AOL, CompuServe, and Prodigy, you can in effect become your own travel agent. Here are some of the things you can do with easySABRE:

- Display a list of all the flights that go to your destination on the date you want to leave.
- Find the cheapest fares based on advance reservations, length of stay, etc.
- Reserve seats on the flight of your choice.
- Pay for the ticket using a credit card.

Suppose you were planning a trip to Hawaii from San Francisco. With easySABRE's FlightFinder feature, you could get information on all flights and fares for the times you wanted to go and return, as shown in this example from Prodigy:

```
PRODIGY® service - EASYSABRE
File  Edit  GoTo  Page  Search  Contents  Goodies  Help
easySABRE (sm)
AVAILABLE FLIGHT OPTIONS

   Flight Date Depart   Arrive     Eqp S
 > CO  89 20MAR SFO 1025A HNL 0145P D10 0
   CO  88 30MAR HNL 0245P SFO 0940P D10 0
               Price Per Person   326.00 USD

 > NW 929 20MAR SFO 1240P HNL 0410P D10 0
   NW 928 30MAR HNL 0540P SFO 1230A D10 0
               Price Per Person   398.00 USD

 > UA 185 20MAR SFO 0130P HNL 0505P D10 0
   UA 184 30MAR HNL 1130P SFO 0616A 757 0
               Price Per Person   432.00 USD
```

Here's how to locate the flight information:

1. Click Travel on the main menu, then choose easySABRE Main Menu under Reservations.

2. Click Reservations and type in your password. (If you aren't already registered to use easySABRE, you'll be prompted to do that first.)

3. Click easySABRE Reservations Menu.

4. Select FlightFinder, and follow the instructions for entering information about where and when you want to fly. That's it. EasySABRE then goes out and gets the information faster than any travel agent.

HOW TO GET RICH

That headline was just to get you to keep reading. In fact, online services offer abundant resources that could help you make successful investments, or at least manage your finances better. If you're like most busy people, you probably follow the stock market—and maybe you even own some shares. Want to see how your stock is doing without having to wait for the morning paper? It's easy. AOL, CompuServe, and Prodigy let you look up stock quotes easily. (MSN doesn't have this feature as of early 1996, but they do say they're working on it.)

In CompuServe, checking out stock prices goes like this:

1. Click the Quotes button on the toolbar. (AOL also has a Quotes button.)

2. Click Add, and type in the ticker symbol of the stock you want to look into.

3. Click Get to see the latest quote. Hmm... from this quote, it appears that America Online's stock is down a tad:

Ticker	Volume	High	Low	Last	Change	Update
amer	10	51.500	51.375	51.375	-0.500	9:25

Stuff for the Serious Investor

Of all the online services, CompuServe offers the widest array of investment tools. Not only can you do near-professional-quality research on companies that you're considering investing in, you can

actually trade stocks online through brokers affiliated with the online services. But remember: Some of these options cost extra.

To access a broker using CompuServe, do the following:

1. Click Finance in the main menu.
2. Click Investing in the Personal Finance Center menu.
3. Click Brokerages, as shown here, to see a list of investment houses that handle online trading:

4. Pick from the list of available brokerages—which includes Quick & Reilly and E*TRADE Securities. You'll see information on how online trading works, and instructions on how to open an account.

A BUILT-IN REFERENCE LIBRARY

Online services give you access to basic reference works, such as encyclopedias, almanacs, and family medical guides. They lack most of the multimedia features of comparable programs that you can buy on CD-ROMs. On the other hand, online information is always current, whereas CD-ROMs, like printed books, get out of date after a while. The biggest advantages of an online reference work, however, are that it doesn't take up any space at all and you always know where to find it.

Microsoft Leverages Its Strength

While the Microsoft Network has its shortcomings—less content than its competitors, and an interface that takes some getting used to—it shines when it comes to reference materials. That's because Microsoft has a way to put its best-selling Encarta multimedia encyclopedia and its impressive Microsoft Bookshelf reference group on MSN.

A Reasonable Facsimile of the Real Thing

You don't get video and animation or long sound clips in the online editions of Encarta and Bookshelf, but they're still impressive. For instance, the online edition of Bookshelf includes the English dictionary, thesaurus, dictionary of quotations, and almanac that come with the CD-ROM version. Furthermore, the online version has the same look and feel as the original. If you want to, you can even search for a topic in all of these works at the same time. Need a short biography of the great Dodger pitcher Sandy Koufax? Here it is, straight out of the online edition of Bookshelf:

Encarta and Bookshelf are not automatically installed when you sign up with the Microsoft Network. You install them online while you're logged onto the service. It takes a few minutes and a modicum of space on your hard disk, but once they're loaded, you can use them anytime you get the urge.

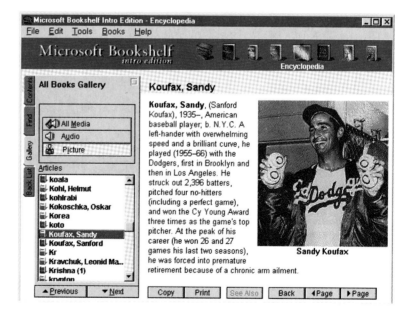

SOFTWARE STOREHOUSES

For those who are more experienced with PCs, online services offer a special treat: software that you can *download* onto your own machine. There are shareware programs and freeware programs. (As defined earlier, shareware is software you're supposed to pay for after a trial period. Freeware is just that: free.) Software available online runs the gamut from complete programs for, say, managing e-mail to little knick-knacks, like a program that displays a cute clock on your PC desktop.

How to Get the Goods

CompuServe and AOL boast extensive software libraries and provide good searching capabilities to help you track down the programs you want. The search feature in AOL is especially user-friendly; in fact, you activate it right from the toolbar.

definition

downloading: Transferring a file from another computer, which can be anywhere in the world, to your PC over a telephone line or other data communications link.

DOWNLOADING SOFTWARE IN AMERICA ONLINE step by step

1. Click the File Search button on the toolbar to bring up the Software Search window.

2. Choose a date range, and select categories to search. Your choices include Windows, DOS, Games, and Graphics & Animation. You can pick more than one category, and the more you choose, the less time the search will take.

3. Click the List Matching Files button to pull up a list of software files that fall into the criteria you've selected. The list doesn't give a lot of information on each file —just the name of the file and the subject it involves. If you need more information, click the Read Description button.

4. If you decide to download a file, highlight it and click the Download Now button.

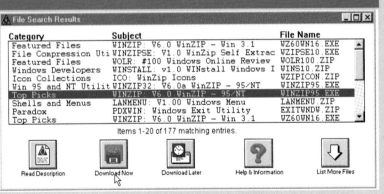

5. You'll be prompted to set a destination folder for the file. Once you've done so, click OK and the download will begin.

Bigger files that you download tend to be compressed (that's zipped in computer-speak, as you'll recall from Chapter 7). Some of these files are self-expanding; they usually have an .exe file extension. But many other compressed files end with .zip. To expand these files, you'll need a zip-unzip program such as WinZip, which you should also be able to download from your online service.

EDUCATION ONLINE

A chief way that online services try luring new subscribers, many of whom have families, is with educational material. In addition to the standard reference works like dictionaries and thesauruses, there are online sections devoted entirely to students—from preschool all the way through college. In fact, AOL even gives you access to The College Board, which provides schedules of college entrance exams and tips for planning your higher education.

Help with Homework

For the younger set, an online service can be a good way to get help with school work. (It also can take some pressure off parents, who may not have lots of time to spend helping their kids with homework assignments.) Prodigy has a feature called Homework Helper that lets students ask questions in their own words, then lists reference materials where the answers can be found. The drawback to Homework Helper is that it doesn't come with Prodigy's basic service, so it costs extra. AOL, on the other hand, has a no-charge service called Homework Help that provides students with links to a number of good reference materials, as you can see here:

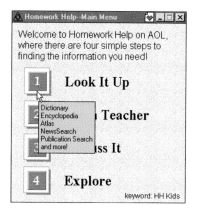

THE COMMUNITY SPIRIT

What really makes online services dynamic are the ways in which they let you interact with other subscribers. In fact, electronic *bulletin boards* and *chat rooms* are among the most popular features of these

bulletin board: An area for reading and posting messages on a given topic, such as gardening, or baseball. Bulletin board *is a generic term that Prodigy happens to use. AOL uses the term* message board, CompuServe just uses message, *and MSN says* BBS.

chat room: An area devoted to live online dialogue with other participants. When you "enter" a chat room, whatever you type appears onscreen in a running commentary—usually on a designated subject. (There also are chat rooms for general discussions on anything that comes to mind, although a busy person might have something better to do than chat for the sake of chatting.)

services, with thousands of people taking part in the electronic exchange of ideas and opinions. Bulletin boards are fundamentally like Internet Newsgroups, except they're limited to the membership of the online service. In the interest of keeping things simple, we'll discuss newsgroups in Chapter 12.

Parental Guidance Suggested

Some bulletin boards and chat rooms deal with sex and other things that you might not want your child exposed to. In light of the current debate over online decency, the big services are taking steps to police themselves. Prodigy and AOL, for example, let you alert the service if you see something objectionable in one of their public areas. There is also a trend toward giving parents the power to limit the material their children can access. AOL now offers a feature called Parental Controls that lets you do just that. Here's how to use it:

1. Click People Connection in AOL's main menu, which takes you to a main Chat lobby.
2. Click the Parental Control button to bring up the following window:

3. You can use the buttons at the lower right of the window to set privileges for chat rooms and Internet newsgroups (which can also be accessed through online services). You may simply choose to restrict your child to the Kids Only section of AOL, which includes Homework Help and some other stuff designed to spark the interest of younger kids.

How About a Nice Chat?

All chat rooms work pretty much the same way: You type in your two cents' worth at the bottom, and then send it along. Your input will appear on the screen, but there often is a delay if a lot of other people are in the room, all trying to talk at once. Also, the more chatters there are, the more disjointed the discussion can get.

Chat rooms can be pretty cool experiences. Online services have rooms for members to gather and discuss current hot-button issues as well as myriad other topics that affect your daily life. For example, in a chat room devoted to PCs you could float a question about a piece of software that isn't working right, and somebody might give you the solution. Rooms on sports and the Internet produce especially lively discussions. It's the kind of stuff you get in a good barroom debate, but without having to go to a bar. In the following illustration, 23 AOL members are embroiled in a raucous discussion about the World Wide Web:

MAIL CALL

If you didn't use any other part of an online service, it still would be worth having just for one thing—electronic mail. E-mail is the single most popular feature of any online service. It lets you send electronic messages anywhere in the world for the price of a local phone call. And while a regular letter might take a week to get to someone in another country, e-mail can take just minutes.

All You Need Is an Address

The great thing about using e-mail is that it isn't necessary for both the sender and the recipient to belong to the same online service. All online services now can route e-mail through the Internet, so you

*You have to be connected to your
online service to send a message
or view new messages you've
received. But you can compose
mail off-line, and then send it
after logging onto your service.
Take advantage of this feature,
because writing letters online
can eat up your free monthly
connect time in a big hurry.*

can correspond with anyone who has an e-mail address, whether the
person is using your online service, a competing service, or an Internet
provider.

Composing an E-Mail Letter

E-mail programs provided by online services share common features;
in fact, they're so similar that if you learn how to use one, you should
have no trouble with another. (To use e-mail in MSN, however, you have
to run Microsoft Exchange, the messaging and fax package that comes
with Windows 95.) The basic e-mail form looks like this—which happens to be the one used by AOL:

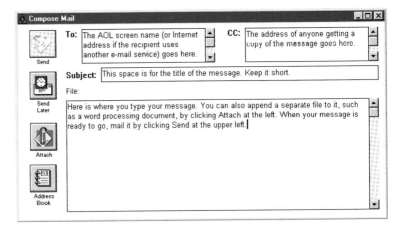

As you can see, the window is broken up into several main parts:

- A place to put the e-mail address of the person you're
  sending the message to
- Room for addresses of other people to whom you want to
  send copies
- Space to type in the subject of your missive
- A main area in which you type the letter itself

Create an Address Book All the online services let you
store names and Internet addresses in an electronic address book. This
saves time when it comes to addressing a message, and also frees you
from having to remember e-mail addresses, which can be really easy
to forget. To create an address book in CompuServe, do the following:

1. Choose Address Book from the Mail menu. Click Add, which brings up this window:

Add to Address Book

Name: Joe Schlobtnick
Address: Joe@Creepco.com
Address Type: Internet
Comments:

[OK] [Cancel] [Help]

2. Type the name of the person, and press TAB.
3. Enter the e-mail address, and pick the type of service (CompuServe, Internet, etc.) from the drop-down Address Type list.
4. Click OK.

Receiving E-Mail

This is the all-time no-brainer. Each time you connect to your online service, it will alert you if you have new mail. CompuServe and AOL even tell you about it using recorded human voices. Here's how the Microsoft Network lets you know you have mail:

If you'd rather not have the computer talk to you, you can turn off the sounds. In AOL, choose Set Preferences from the Members menu, click the General icon, and deselect the Enable Events Sound box. In CompuServe, choose Session Settings from the Special menu, click Modem, and select the Speaker Off box.

The Microsoft Network

File   Edit   View   Tools   Help

The Microsoft Network

MSN TODAY

E-MAIL

The Microsoft Network

You have received new mail on The Microsoft Network.

[OK]

FAVO

MEMB

CATEGORIES

Welcome to MSN Central.

All the online services let you

save your incoming mail, as well

as messages you send, for future

reference. It's a good idea to

hang onto important mail,

particularly for keeping track of

an ongoing correspondence.

Reading Your E-Mail

The process is similar in all of the online services. In CompuServe, for instance, use the following steps to view new mail:

1. Choose Get New Mail from the Mail menu to see a list of new messages.

2. To open a message, either double-click on it, or click once to highlight it and then click the Get button. (If you have only one new message, it will automatically be highlighted, in which case you can just click Get.) The message then appears, as in this example:

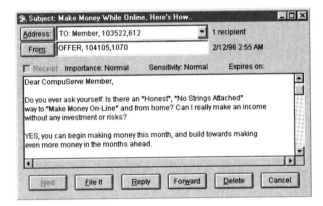

Even e-mail can turn out to be junk mail, as you can see in the case here—an unsolicited message touting a get-rich-quick scheme.

ON TO THE INTERNET

For years, online services battled primarily against each other. Today, however, they have a common adversary—the Internet. To keep pace, AOL, CompuServe, Prodigy, and MSN are all offering Internet access and integrating their own features with those available on the Internet. Without further ado, let's take a look at the Internet—a global phenomenon that some people are calling "the mother of all networks."

Internet: The Mother of All Networks

FAST FORWARD

CHANGE THE STARTUP PAGE
FOR YOUR WEB BROWSER ➤ *p. 260*

Netscape Navigator takes you to Netscape Communications' home page when you first connect to the Internet. But you can have it start with any page you want—say Yahoo, or one of the other directories that help you find your way around the Web.

1. From the Options menu, choose General Preferences.
2. Click the Appearance tab, then type in the address of the Web site you want as your browser's *home page.*
3. Click OK. Next time you start up Navigator, the first thing you'll see is your new page.

USE A DIRECTORY TO
NAVIGATE THE WEB ➤ *pp. 262-263*

There are several powerful directories on the Web that contain links to thousands of Web sites. Leading search services include Yahoo, Infoseek, Magellan, and Excite—all of which you can use for free.

1. Access one of the services. They're easily reached through either the Netscape home page or the Microsoft Network page, which is the default startup page for the latest version of Microsoft's browser.
2. To use a directory, click one of the subjects, such as Entertainment or Government. That will take you to another directory with more choices. You'll be amazed at some of the stuff you can find this way.
3. If you know exactly what you're looking for, you can search using words or phrases.

DOWNLOAD A FILE ➤ *pp. 267-268*

1. Find the downloadable file you want—the latest version of Netscape Navigator, for instance. Go to the Netscape home page and follow the directions to locate the file.
2. Click the link that starts the download.
3. In the Save As box that appears, make sure the filename and destination folder are okay. (You can change the folder, but it's better to leave the filename unchanged.)
4. Click Save to start the download.

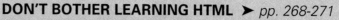

DON'T BOTHER LEARNING HTML ➤ *pp. 268-271*

Web pages are written in a special programming language called HTML, but you can create your own page without knowing a lick of it. Use a program like Microsoft's Internet Assistant, which lets you build a simple but effective home page from within Word for Windows 95, using familiar Windows tools.

SET UP YOUR E-MAIL PROGRAM ➤ *pp. 273-274*

Eudora Light, a free program that you can download on the Web, is the most popular e-mail software around. And it's easy to set up for use with your Internet account:

1. Choose Settings from the Special menu to display the Settings window.
2. Use the category icons that run down the left side to fill in information Eudora needs to connect with your Internet provider. You'll need your e-mail address, your POP account, and the address of your SMTP server. (Ask your provider if you don't know.)

USE NETSCAPE TO ACCESS NEWSGROUPS ➤ *pp. 277-281*

1. Configure Netscape Navigator so it can access newsgroups.
2. Choose Mail and News Preferences from the Options menu, tab over to Servers, and enter the name of your Internet provider's news server in the space labeled News (NTTP) Server.
3. Click OK.
4. After connecting to the Internet, choose Netscape News from the Window menu.

In 1993, the San Francisco Chronicle, which follows the technology business closely, carried 35 articles about the Internet. The following year, the number grew to 252. And in 1995, it leaped to 887—better than two a day. By the beginning of 1996, the Internet was the hottest area of consumer technology, with young companies like Netscape Communications—as well as leviathans like Microsoft and AT&T—fueling the market for Internet products and services. For PC users, the Internet is changing from a novelty into a necessity.

A COMPUTING CORNUCOPIA

The Internet has been around for more than two decades. It was devised to link U.S. government agencies and universities so that vital communications wouldn't be cut off in the event of a nuclear war. Over the years, the Internet grew to become a global computer network; however, it wasn't until the emergence of the *World Wide Web* in the last few years that it began to catch on with the public. And boy, did it catch on! Today, millions of people use the Internet on a regular basis to:

- Access the Web, which now boasts hundreds of thousands of *sites* around the world operated by governments, universities, businesses, and individuals. The range of material to be found on the Web is virtually unlimited. If you can think of a subject, there's probably a Web site devoted to it.
- Send and receive e-mail. Using the Internet, you can send a message to anyone anywhere who also has an e-mail address, and most people can do it with a local phone call—in other words, for free.
- Participate in newsgroups. These are electronic bulletin boards on thousands of topics that let you read and post messages to other people with similar interests.

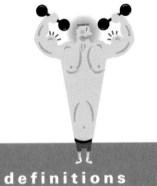

definitions

World Wide Web: A global subset of the Internet that presents information graphically. The Web connects Net information using special links that you activate with your mouse.

Web site: A location on the World Wide Web. Businesses, government agencies, universities, nonprofits, clubs, and even individuals have created sites. (Of course, Web sites aren't physical places. They're located inside computers!)

All Roads Lead to the Internet

With the explosion in the demand for Internet services, everybody seems to be getting into the act. All of the commercial online services now offer access to the Web, e-mail, and newsgroups. In fact, as we saw in the last chapter, e-mail is one of the most widely used features of companies like America Online and CompuServe. However, this chapter assumes you have a direct dial-up account with an Internet service provider. If you don't, see Chapter 10 for information on how to get connected.

WEB BROWSERS

What really kicked the World Wide Web into high gear was the development of *browsers*—software for navigating the Web. Browsers give PC users the ability to point and click their way around individual Web sites and between different sites. You can even leap between two sites halfway around the world without even realizing you've done it. Browsers also give you access to parts of the Internet that aren't on the Web, including University mainframes that hold tons of downloadable software.

If You're Browsing, You're Probably Using Netscape

As I write this, the most popular Web browser by far is Netscape Navigator, which you can take a look at in Figure 12.1. By literally giving its browsers away, Netscape has succeeded in capturing more than three-fourths of the nascent market. Netscape has held that market by staying ahead of the technology curve at every turn, adding new features and improving the Navigator with several upgrades.

Watch Out—Here Comes Microsoft

Just because Netscape owns the market doesn't mean you have no other choices. There are other excellent browsers out there. Not surprisingly, one of them comes from Microsoft, whose Internet Explorer browser is starting to gain a following. This is in no small part because, like Netscape, Microsoft is giving its browser away at every opportunity. (For example, it comes with the Microsoft Plus! add-on

Menu bar

Toolbar

Location

Text hyperlinks

Status bar

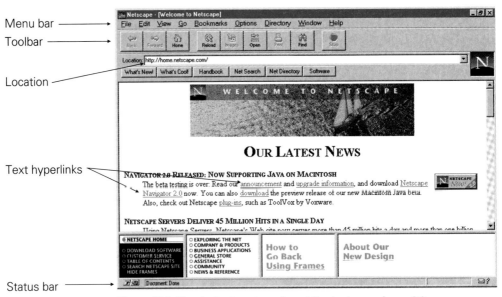

Figure 12.1 Here's the latest version of Navigator—release 2.0.

You're probably wondering how a company like Netscape can make money if it gives its products away. The answer is that they sell software to businesses that want to set up and administer Web sites—there's a lot more profit in that than there would be in marketing browsers, which are fairly simple programs.

package for Windows 95.) In addition, starting this summer, Internet Explorer will become the standard Web browser built into America Online's software. As you can see here, the Internet Explorer 2.0 looks very similar to the Netscape Navigator.

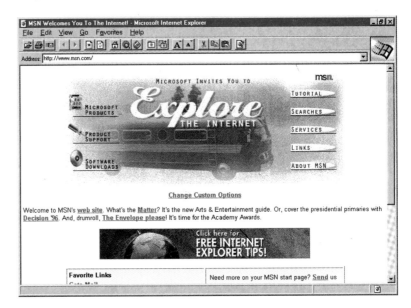

Both Netscape and Microsoft let you download the latest versions of their browsers for free, right off their Web sites. (You'll learn how to download files a little later.) Make it a point to check these sites regularly—it's an easy way to guarantee that you have the latest browser. Just to be safe, you might consider keeping two browsers on your system so that if one stops working, you'll have a way to download a replacement for it using the other browser.

The fact is, all browsers look pretty much alike on the outside, so you should be able to use any major browser with any direct dial-up connection to the Internet.

So What's the Difference?

Although they all work the same way, each browser has a few unique features and uses technology that differentiates it a little from the competition. As a result, a Web site created to take advantage of Netscape Navigator may not look as snappy when viewed with a competitive browser. (The same holds true for Microsoft's Internet Explorer.) As technology continues to evolve, one browser may gain a clear-cut advantage, or they may all end up adhering to the same standards. Right now, Netscape seems to have the advantage. For one thing, it's the first browser to support a new technology in which web pages are divided into *frames*, which make it easier to navigate through a Web site. In the following example, the Web search service Infoseek lets you click search options in one frame (on the left), and have the results appear in another (at the right):

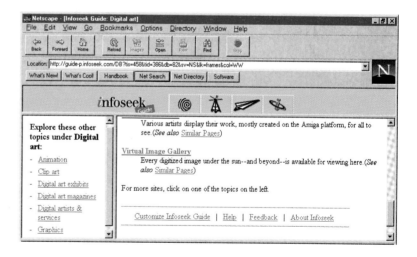

ANATOMY OF A WEB SITE

A World Wide Web site is sort of like a digital book. It consists of electronic pages, starting off with what's called a *home page*. For some sites, the book starts and ends at the home page, which can consist of

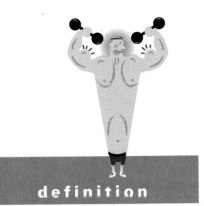

page: A single file of information on a Web site. A page can be short, consisting of a few lines of text and a graphic image—or so long that you have to scroll down several screens full of stuff to see the whole thing.

just a few lines of text and a graphic image. Many corporate sites, however, have dozens of pages nestled behind elaborately illustrated home pages, full of information about products and services.

Browsers Have Home Pages Too (but You Can Change Them)

By default, Netscape Navigator loads the Netscape Communications home page when it first connects to your Internet service. Likewise, Internet Explorer takes you straight to the Web site for the Microsoft Network. But you can set your browser to display any page you want on startup. Here's how to do it with Netscape:

1. Choose General Preferences from the Options menu.
2. Click the Appearance tab, if necessary, and then type in a new address in the Start With box, as shown here:

![Preferences dialog box showing the Appearance tab with Toolbars, Startup, and Link Styles sections. The Home Page Location field shows http://home.netscape.com/]

The Home button on a browser's toolbar doesn't take you back to the home page of a Web site you're visiting. It takes you back to the startup page for your browser.

3. Click OK. The next time you start Navigator, your new startup page will appear.

YOUR LINKS TO THE WORLD

What makes the Web special is that it gives you the ability to go from place to place just by clicking your mouse, using what's called hypertext links. Either text or images can serve as these *hyperlinks*. Text links are easily identified because they are underlined and/or a different color (usually blue). You'll also know that text or an image is a link if the mouse pointer turns into a hand, like this:

When you click on a link, it can take you elsewhere within the Web site you're visiting, or it can transport you to another site somewhere else—anywhere in the world, depending on where the link is directed. This ability to connect far-flung computers in a matter of seconds is why they call it the World Wide Web.

http://www.confusing.com

Every one of the hundreds of thousands of Web sites in the world has a unique *address* (called a *location* by Netscape) so it can be located by other computers on the Internet. And every page within every site also has its own address, which is an extended version of the site's address. Web addresses also are known as URLs (for *Universal Resource Locators*). A typical address might look like this:

```
http://www.yahoo.com
```

Here's a breakdown of what it means:

http Stands for *HyperText Transfer Protocol*, which is the standard for transmitting Web pages across the Internet.

www *World Wide Web.* That one's obvious.

yahoo The name of the company or organization operating the site. Yahoo is a company that provides an Internet directory and search service.

com Denotes what kind of site it is. *The com* extension is used for corporations and businesses. Other tags include *edu* for educational institutions, and *gov* for government agencies.

habits & strategies

Don't worry too much about addresses. Most of the time, you can move from place to place on the Web without even being aware of addresses. That's because when you click on a link, you're automatically directed to the address of the linked page, whether it's at the same site or a separate one.

Nobody's Perfect—Not Even the Web

There will be times when you just can't connect to a site. This could happen for a number of reasons:

- The address you're using may be wrong, or the site you're trying to reach may have changed its address or even gone out of business.
- The server that hosts the site may be temporarily down.
- All the lines going into the site may be busy.

If your browser can't make a connection to the site, you'll usually get an error message like this one:

As a general rule, if your browser doesn't connect to a site within a minute or two, it probably ain't gonna happen. When you get tired of waiting, click the Stop button on the toolbar, and try another link or site.

> **Netscape**
>
> ⚠ There was no response. The server could be down or is not responding.
>
> If you are unable to connect again later, contact the server's administrator.
>
> [OK]

CONDUCTING A SEARCH

Finding a particular Web site if you don't know its address could be a real needle-in-the-haystack affair. Fortunately, there are a number of popular Web directories and search services that let you ferret out sites fairly easily.

- *Directories* are lists of categories of subjects. Each category could contain several sub-categories, allowing you to focus your search, until finally you arrive at a list of actual Web sites for a specific topic.
- *Search services* let you enter words or combinations of words, and then go out and find sites that match your search.

Several companies have combined directory and search capabilities. The best of these are Infoseek, Magellan, Excite, and Yahoo. You can check out Yahoo's main screen by looking up ahead there:

Find a Page You Like?
Create a Bookmark!

Suppose you find a Web page you really find fascinating,—one you'd like to revisit in the future. Then suppose it has an address as long as your arm. Take this one for example, which is the address for the home page of the White House:

```
http://www2.whitehouse.gov/WH/Welcome.html
```

Nobody in his right mind would write that down, let alone memorize it. But there's an easy way to store addresses using a feature called Bookmarks in Netscape Navigator, and Favorites in Microsoft Internet Explorer. The process is the same in either browser. First, load the Web page whose address you want to save. Then choose Add Bookmark from the Bookmarks menu in Netscape, or Add to Favorites in the Favorites menu of Internet Explorer. Next time you want to access the page, open the menu and click on the name of the page, as shown in the following example from Internet Explorer:

The Direct Approach

If you know the address of a site but haven't created a bookmark for it, you can still go directly to it by one of these methods:

- Enter the address in the Address box beneath the browser's toolbar (the Location box in Netscape), and press ENTER. (Don't worry about capitalization; the Internet isn't case-sensitive when it comes to recognizing addresses.)
- Click the Open button on the toolbar, which in Netscape displays the following box:

Simply type in the address and press ENTER.

You Gotta Have the Moves

Once you've begun browsing, Netscape Navigator and other browsers store pages you visit during an online session in a *history*.

CAUTION

If you go backward in a history, and then take off in a new direction, the history's path is altered. The old history is erased from that point forward and replaced with the new one you create. This is a good reason not to rely on the history feature too much. It also might be an argument against time travel...who knows?

This handy feature lets you quickly revisit pages without having to load them again. To go back to the most recently viewed page, click the Back button on the toolbar. Clicking the Forward button takes you to the next page in the history. The buttons only move you one page at a time. To go straight to a page in the history in Netscape Navigator, open the Go menu, as seen here, and click on the page you want. (In Internet Explorer, you'll find the history at the bottom of the File menu.)

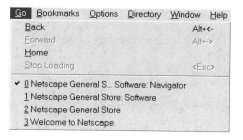

Stop Right There!

Suppose you're loading a Web page, and it's taking forever. Or you decide that's not really where you want to be. No problem. Just click the Stop button on the toolbar, which halts the loading process dead in its tracks and lets you do something else.

MAKING YOUR BROWSER WORK FOR YOU

Browsers designed for Windows 95—including Netscape Navigator 2.0 and Microsoft Internet Explorer 2.0—are highly integrated with the operating system. As a result, you can copy, save, and print information from a Web site just as you would using another program like a word processor.

Printing, Copying, and Saving Text

Let's say that in your travels around the Web you come upon an interesting article on health or information about a new video game your son wants you to buy.

SHORTCUT

One of the best uses of the copying function is to copy Web addresses, which have to be entered exactly or they don't work. Suppose you come across a news article while browsing that includes a lengthy address. To open the Web site, copy the address and then paste it into the Location or Address box. Cool!

- To print the article and have it appear the way it does on the screen, click the Print button on the browser's toolbar. That will bring up the Print dialog box. Click OK to print.
- If you want to copy the article, choose Select All from the Edit menu, then choose Copy from the same menu. If you don't want the whole article, highlight the part you want with your mouse, and then choose Copy from the Edit menu. Start your word processor, and choose Paste from its Edit menu to insert the copied text.
- To save an entire Web page, choose Save As from the browser's File menu. You can save the page either as simple text, or as HTML, which will enable you to view the page in the future with a browser. (What does HTML mean? We'll get to that later.)

Copying and Saving Images

Using Microsoft's browser, you can copy an image the same way you would copy text (this is one advantage Microsoft has over Netscape, which doesn't let you copy images). Either browser allows you to save an image as a graphics file. Right-click the image, then choose the Save function from the shortcut menu, shown here in Netscape:

Back in Frame
Forward in Frame

View this Image (home_igloo.jpg)
Save this Image as...
Copy this Image Location
Load this Image

Internet Shortcut

You can save both regular images, and images that serve as links. Some images are in GIF format; others are in JPEG, which uses greater compression to reduce the size of the file. Once an image is saved, you can keep it and use it in any program capable of using the graphics format of the image.

DOWNLOADING FROM THE WEB

The Internet is a virtual treasure-trove of software—both share-ware and freeware—that you can download and install on your PC. Many of those programs can be found in huge software libraries in mainframe computers, mostly at universities. In addition, some software companies offer useful programs that you can download from their home pages. To illustrate the process of downloading, let's go after a program called Internet Assistant from Microsoft—a free add-on to Word for Windows 95. It's a program that lets you create your own home page on the Web—which just happens to be the topic of the next section of this chapter.

First, Find the File...

For this example, I went to the Microsoft home page at http://www.microsoft.com. I clicked on a link labeled "Products," which took me to a list that included a link labeled "Internet Assistant for Word 95". Aha! That's what I wanted to download. From here, I proceeded through a couple more linked pages, which explained the program and how to install it once the download is finished.

Finally I got to a page with a link saying, "OK, download Internet Assistant now!" I used Netscape to do the job. (Didn't want to show too much favoritism toward Microsoft.) I clicked on the link, and a Save As dialog box appeared, as shown in Figure 12.2.

I clicked the Save button to begin the download. A box appeared showing the progress of the download—how big the file was, how fast it was transferred to my PC, and approximately how much time remained at any given moment before the process would finish. When the download was complete, the status box disappeared.

Once You've Downloaded, Then What?

Most programs that you download consist of several files crammed into one compressed file (a compressed file takes up less space, so it downloads faster). Before you can install the program, you have to decompress the file—a process that extracts all the files within the original, blows them up to normal size, and places them in the same folder as the compressed file. There are two kinds of compressed files:

SHORTCUT

Names are automatically assigned both to the file you're downloading, and to the folder where it will be saved. You can change either one of these names if you want, but it's usually a good idea to leave the filename unchanged. That way you'll be able to recognize it easily if the file is referred to in any documentation you end up consulting later on. Besides, why should a busy person spend more time than necessary thinking up filenames?

Figure 12.2 It's a snap to download files with Netscape.

Create a separate folder to use for saving files when you download them. This will help you easily keep track of any files that are extracted when you decompress a downloaded file.

- Some have .zip file extensions. To decompress one of these, you'll need a utility like WinZip. (See Chapter 7 for a description of WinZip—which, by the way, you can also download. To find a copy, search for the word "WinZip" using a search tool like Infoseek or Yahoo.)
- Other compressed files have .exe extensions. These files decompress themselves when you double-click them. Some of them, like the file for Internet Assistant, even automatically begin the installation process.

Installing a Downloaded Program

With most downloads, you'll have to manually install the program. Here's how: In Windows Explorer, locate the installation file (usually setup.exe or install.exe) among the files that were extracted during decompression. Double-click the file and follow the instructions that appear.

CREATING YOUR OWN WEB PAGE

Web pages are built using HTML, which, as noted earlier, stands for *Hypertext Markup Language*. It isn't an especially difficult programming language, but if you're a busy person, you really won't have time to learn it. That's where a program like Internet Assistant for Word for

CAUTION

You can't have a home page on the Web unless you have a permanent Web address so that other people on the Internet will be able to find you—and a dial-up Internet account doesn't usually give you an address. You can have your provider assign you one, but it will cost extra.

Windows 95 comes in. It works from within the word processing program, letting you use familiar Windows tools to create Web pages. (There are several other similar programs for easily building Web pages, and Netscape's commercially available Netscape Navigator Gold lets you write HTML directly in the browser.) Once you've installed Internet Assistant, here's how to start building a Web page:

1. Launch Word for Windows 95 and choose New from the File menu.
2. Double-click the Html.dot icon. This will bring up a blank page with the Internet Assistant menus and toolbars:

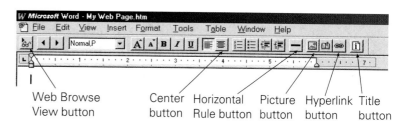

Web Browse View button Center button Horizontal Rule button Picture button Hyperlink button Title button

A Few Basics to Get You Started

First thing to do is give your page a title. This won't show up in the page itself, but whatever you type as the title will appear in the title bar of a browser viewing your page. You get up to 64 characters. Click the Title button on the toolbar and enter your title. Once you've done that, you can start building your page. First thing should be a catchy headline:

1. Click your text insertion point at the start of the page, then open the Style list and choose Heading 1,H1:

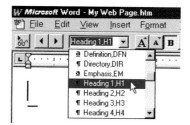

2. Type your headline, which will appear in the type style and size normally used for the top headline on a Web page.

SHORTCUT

You don't have to start a browser and load your Web page to see how it will look on the Web. Instead, just click the Web Browse View button on the toolbar. (The only reason I used Netscape was to make it look super authentic.)

3. With the insertion point anywhere in the headline, click the Center button on the toolbar to center it between the left and right edges of the page.
4. Just for fun, let's put a horizontal rule beneath the headline to set it off from the rest of the page. At the end of the title, press ENTER to move the insertion point down.
5. To add the line, click the Horizontal Rule button on the toolbar.

Add an Image to Jazz Up the Page

You can use any JPEG or GIF image to dress up your page. (JPEG takes longer to appear, but usually looks sharper.) You can use images from a clip art collection, or a photo or drawing you've scanned. If you use scanned art, you'll have to convert it from the standard scanning format, called TIFF. (In this instance I got lazy, so I just stole the main graphic off of the Microsoft Network site, saving it to a file on my PC.) To place the image on your Web page, click the insertion point where you want it to go, then click the Picture button on the toolbar. Use the browse button to find the image, and then click OK. After inserting the image, center it using the Center button.

And Finally, the Magic Ingredient— A Hyperlink

A Web page wouldn't be a Web page without hyperlinks. It's common practice to have links that take you to other pages at your site, as well as to different sites altogether. Once you've typed in some text, highlight the words that you want to serve as the link. Then click the Hyperlink button on the toolbar, and enter the Internet address that the link will take you to. For this example, I linked to http://www.msn.com (the Microsoft Network). To see my new Web page, including the headline, graphical image, and hyperlink, check out Figure 12.3.

You're On Your Own Now

There are all sorts of things you can put into your Web page, such as bulleted lists and different kinds of headlines. For some good tips, switch to Web Browse view and click the Home button on the toolbar, which takes you to the Internet Assistant home page (it's downloaded along with the program). Good luck!

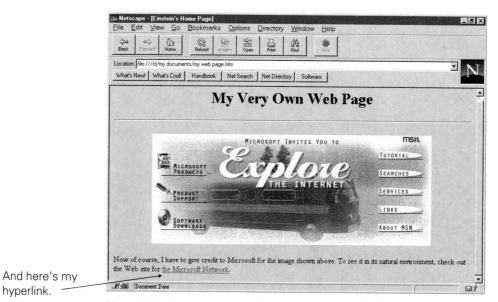

And here's my hyperlink.

Figure 12.3 Here's my sample Web page, as viewed in Netscape Navigator.

E-MAIL—THE PC TOOL THAT'S MAKING STAMPS OBSOLETE

When Thomas Jefferson was president, someone once asked him about his minister to Spain. Jefferson was said to have replied "I haven't heard from him in two years. If I do not hear from him next year, I will write him a letter." If e-mail had existed back then, Jefferson could have done a much better job of keeping the silent diplomat on his toes:

With your PC, and an Internet connection, you can send an electronic letter anywhere in the world in a matter of minutes. Not surprisingly, more and more people are using e-mail instead of regular mail, since it's faster, plus you don't have to lick the envelope.

As you saw in the Chapter 11, e-mail has become a popular feature of online services such as America Online and CompuServe. But an Internet account is just as effective for e-mail, and some Internet software outstrips online services in the ability to handle and sort messages.

Pick Your Own Postman

Two of the best Internet e-mail programs are Qualcomm's Eudora, which is the most widely used of all e-mail packages, and the e-mail feature built into the latest version of Netscape's Web browser. There are two versions of Eudora: Eudora Pro, a fully featured program you can buy at a software store, and Eudora Light, which lacks some of the more advanced features—like the ability to filter incoming messages according to subject or author. But Eudora Light has something else going for it: it's free. You can download it off the Web by going to Qualcomm's site at

```
http://www.qualcomm.com/quest/
```

The Netscape Advantage

By building e-mail right into its browser, Netscape has given itself a major advantage over separate e-mail programs. If you're surfing the Web and you decide to check your mail or send a message, all you have to do is choose Netscape Mail from the Windows menu, as shown here, and you'll be switched to e-mail.

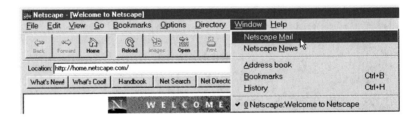

By comparison, you have to start Eudora Light separately while you're logged onto the Internet.

Setting Up Your E-Mail Program

Before you can send and receive messages, you have to set up your e-mail program to work with your Internet account. For this you'll need several pieces of information:

Your E-Mail Address This consists of the name you use to sign onto your Internet account and the name of your Internet host (the computer used by your Internet provider), separated by the @ sign. For instance:

    Jim@nethost.com

Your POP Account This is usually the same as your Internet address.

Your SMTP Server Ordinarily, this is just the host name.

The best plan is to consult your Internet service provider and get all this information before setting up your mail program.

Configuring Eudora Light

Choose Settings from the Special menu to display the Settings window. You'll see some colorful category icons down the left side. Select the top icon, Getting Started, and fill in the form, as shown here. (Use your own information, though!)

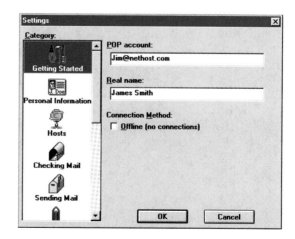

definitions

POP: Post Office Protocol. *The format that e-mail programs use to retrieve and store messages.*

SMTP: Simple Mail Transport Protocol. *The standard technology for sending messages through the Internet.*

You'll notice that the program asks you to enter your real name in addition to your e-mail address. This is so that when you send a message, your real name will appear in it, and people won't have to try to identify you by a cryptic e-mail address.

273

Next, go to the Personal Information category and fill in your e-mail return address, which should be the same as your POP account. Then go to the Hosts category and enter your SMTP information. (There are more categories and a lot of options, but for a busy person who wants to get moving fast, that's all you need to do.)

Configuring Netscape Navigator

To set up Netscape's browser for e-mail, start by choosing Mail and News Preferences from the Options menu. Then click the Servers tab to bring up this window:

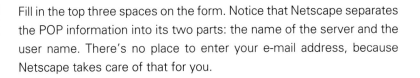

Fill in the top three spaces on the form. Notice that Netscape separates the POP information into its two parts: the name of the server and the user name. There's no place to enter your e-mail address, because Netscape takes care of that for you.

Sending an E-Mail Message

To compose a new message in Navigator, click the New Message button (it's actually labeled To:Mail) on the toolbar. In Eudora Light, there's also a New Message toolbar button: the second one from the left. In the window where you compose mail, you'll follow the same routine as for creating e-mail in online services. (If you need help with this procedure, you can refer back to Chapter 10.)

habits & strategies

E-mail programs like Eudora and Netscape let you do your letter writing off-line, when you're not connected to the Internet. This can save you money if your account provides limited free access time.

Here is the main window in Eudora:

The main window in an e-mail program always includes the following:

- A space for the address of the recipient
- A space labeled cc: for the address of anyone you want to send copies to
- The subject of the message
- An option for attaching a file, such as a word processing document, to your message
- A main writing area for the message itself
- A Send button

Keeping Copies of Your Messages

By default, most e-mail programs keep copies of messages you send, so you can refer to them later. in Netscape, they go into the Sent folder, while Eudora puts them in the Out file. Both programs also let you put messages you no longer want into Trash, which you can empty whenever you feel like it.

Receiving E-Mail

When someone sends you an e-mail message, it doesn't go directly into your PC. Instead, it's sent to the server of your Internet provider, where it stays until you fish it off. You do that by telling your e-mail program to check for mail. (Most programs make you type in your

SHORTCUT

Both Eudora and Netscape let you store names of frequently used e-mail addresses—a feature you should definitely take advantage of so that you don't have to remember addresses and type them in each time you send a message.

password before they'll connect to the server.) If the program finds new mail, it will place it in an In box.

To illustrate this, I've just checked my mail using Eudora Light. Here's today's mail:

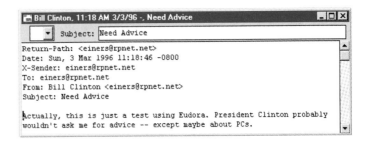

My my, aren't we popular with the cream of society! (Well...here's a confession: I actually changed the Real Name option in Eudora's setup to make it look like these people had written to me.) Anyway, to read a message, just double-click it, which produces this view:

Replying to a Message

One of the really great things about e-mail is that you can exchange messages with someone about a particular subject, going back and forth as many times as you want while using the original message as the basis for your dialog. Some people play chess this way, exchanging moves via e-mail. To answer a message in either Netscape or Eudora, press the Reply button on the toolbar. A new, pre-addressed message composition window will appear. If you want, you can include the text from the original message in your reply. (Each line of the original may be preceded by a >, as in the following example. This format lets you easily distinguish the original message from your reply.)

habits & strategies

You can erase all or part of the original message when you compose your reply, but it's a good idea to leave at least part of it. That way, the other person will know you're replying to a message they sent. If you don't include the original message, your reply can appear meaningless.

```
Netscape - [Re: Belated greetings]                          _ □ ✕
File   Edit   View   Options   Window
                                                              N
Send  Quote  Attach Address    Stop

Mail To:   evans@nethost.com
Cc:
Subject:   Re: Chance to Meet
Attachment:

David Evans wrote:
>
> I'll be in SF 3/19-3/22 for the Icon awards; could get together
> then....?

Sure, I'm free for lunch any of those days. Let me know. Cheers.
```

To include original text in replies using Netscape 2.0, choose Mail and News Preferences from the Options menu, click the Composition tab, and check the box labeled "Automatically quote original message when replying."

Forwarding a Message Suppose you receive a message that you want to share with another person. Say, for example, your brother e-mails you a funny story, and you want to send it to your father. No problem. Just select the message in the In Box directory, press the Forward button on the toolbar, and fill in the e-mail address for dad. Then click Send.

NEWSGROUPS— HIGH-TECH, GLOBAL GOSSIP

Pick a subject. Any subject. There's probably an Internet newsgroup devoted to it. Newsgroups are electronic discussion groups where you read and post messages that can be read and responded to by millions of other people who are also interested in the same topic. As of this writing, there are literally thousands of newsgroups. And the best part is, they're free, and you can access them through your Web browser. The latest version of Netscape Navigator, for instance, has a very slick newsgroup feature called Netscape News.

Before you can gain access to newsgroups, you have to let your browser know the name of the news server used by your Internet provider. (The *news server* is a computer that provides access to newsgroups. Usually, its name consists of the host server name, preceded by the word news—*news.nethost.com,* for instance. The news server is also known as the *NNTP server.*)

SETTING UP NAVIGATOR TO ACCESS NEWSGROUPS step by step

1. From the Options menu in Navigator, choose Mail and News Preferences.
2. Tab over to the Server page.
3. Move on down to the News section, and enter the name of your news server in the appropriate space.
4. Click OK.
5. You're in business! Now to start tapping into those newsgroups, select Netscape News from Navigator's Window menu.

Remember—as with e-mail, you have to be connected directly to the Internet before you can access newsgroups.

With Thousands of Newsgroups, Where Do You Start?

The best way I know is to use one of the Web search directories that also catalogues newsgroups. These include Infoseek and Excite. Type in the subject you're interested in, and the search engine will display any groups that seem to fit. If you're so inclined, you can also display all the newsgroups available through your Internet provider by choosing Show All Newsgroups in the Options menu of the Netscape News window.

definition

NNTP: Network News Transfer Protocol. *This is a computer term. It does not refer to a television news anchor moving from one station to another. It also is the last definition in this book, thank goodness.*

What's with All These Alts, Recs, and Comps?

The first thing you'll notice is that newsgroups have funny names that look kind of like e-mail addresses, but without the @. A typical newsgroup might carry the name rec.music.classical. But there's a method to this madness. To give some sense of organization to newsgroups, they are categorized into areas of broad interest, which are denoted by the first part of a newsgroup's name. Any group beginning with the letters comp, for instance, has to do with computers. Here's a short list of some of the key designators and what they mean:

alt Alternative groups on a variety of topics. The real raunchy sex groups that the government is so heated about are in this category.

biz Business stuff.

comp Computers, including hardware and software.

rec Recreational subjects, including games, hobbies, art, and music.

soc Groups dealing with social issues.

misc Miscellaneous groups that don't really fit anywhere else.

Perusing the Newsgroups with Netscape

The newsgroup window in Netscape 2.0 is divided into three frames, as you can see in Figure 12.4. At the upper left is a list of newsgroups. The upper-right frame is for listing messages in a specific newsgroup. And the frame that comprises the lower part of the screen shows the text of a selected message.

In this case, I selected the rec.animals.wildlife newsgroup by clicking on its name. This produced the rather beastly list of messages you see at the right, and when I clicked one of them, the message itself appeared at the bottom. (It seems we've happened upon an unbridled exchange involving one of the finer points of the English language.)

How to Subscribe to a Newsgroup

Click the box to the right of the name of the newsgroup. (You may have to widen the left frame of the window in order to see the box. You can do this by clicking on the border that separates the left and right frames

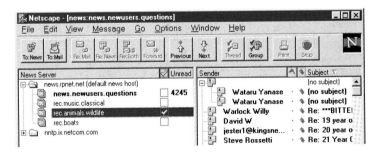

Figure 12.4 Here's what it looks like when you've got all three frames working at the same time.

Notice how the list of messages in the right pane resembles the tree-like way in which folders are displayed in Windows Explorer? What's happened is that Netscape has grouped messages on the same topic together, with responses following the original posting. This threading of messages makes it a lot easier to follow a train of thought within a newsgroup.

and dragging it to the right.) Clicking on the box inserts a yellow check, as shown here, which means you're all signed up. Actually, nobody but you is going to know you've subscribed—but keeping a record is helpful when you want to list only those groups that you've subscribed to. (Use the Options menu for this and other ways of listing groups.)

How to Get Into the Act

Here are some of the ways you can get involved in a newsgroup:

- Post a new message for everyone to see.

- Post a reply to a message someone else has posted.
- Send someone a personal reply, without posting it to the newsgroup.
- Send someone a personal reply and also post it to the newsgroup.

You can do all that stuff by using the buttons on the toolbar in the Netscape News window.

IN THE NAME OF DECENCY

In 1995, a debate began about decency on the Internet. The particular focus was newsgroups, some of which feature highly explicit sexual discussions as well as downloadable photos that would make Hugh Hefner blush. The U.S. government is mulling ways to keep the Internet safe for kids without impeding on the First Amendment. It's a tough task. In the meantime, however, some entrepreneurial software companies have developed programs such as SurfWatch and Cyber Patrol that can help parents by blocking out offensive Web sites and newsgroups.

Always on the Alert

One of the leading programs is SurfWatch, from SurfWatch Software. Once installed, it refers to its built-in listings to prevent anyone who's using the PC from accessing a naughty newsgroup or Web site. With SurfWatch on the case, if you try to load *Playboy* magazine's Web site on your browser, here's what you'll get instead:

SurfWatch can be turned off by use of a password that you specify when you first install the program. Without the password, it's almost impossible to disable the program without wiping out your entire system.

CAUTION

Just because you buy a program like SurfWatch doesn't mean you're safe forever. With new Internet sites coming online every day, there's bound to be some you don't want your kids to see. To keep your electronic sentry up to date, you'll have to pay for regular updates of blocked sites—which you can usually get online from the company that sold you the software.

You also need the password to completely remove SurfWatch from your PC, using the Uninstall feature that comes with it.

OTHER INTERNET ACTION

Hopefully, this chapter has given you a pretty good elementary course on the World Wide Web, e-mail, and newsgroups. The Internet has lots more to offer, with names like FTP, Telnet, Gopher, and IRC. At some point you're probably going to want to know about that stuff. When you do, go out and get Christian Crumlish's *The Internet for Busy People,* another of the colorful and informative books in the Busy People series from Osborne/McGraw-Hill.

Index

N